D1362888

Contents

I'm daunted by the garden I've inherited

In brief:
Make your mark, without throwing the baby out with the bathwater

It is a curious fact that people often keep things they don't like, just because they've always been there. This makes no sense in the case of plants that are not in the least bit special, or, worse, that are a menace. However, just because something is a bit large and unfamiliar, try not to look at it with murder in mind. Have a think; read about it. See if anyone else grows it well. Perhaps it just needs a heavy prune.

Gardens that have been pampered by earlier owners have also had thought and knowledge invested in them. The aesthetic might be wrong for you, but in the new, improved context you are hoping to create, certain things might just work. It's important to remember that large shrubs and trees will give weight to your garden. If you rip them all out in a fit of minimalism, you may find yourself having to buy in fast-growing things because suddenly your new garden looks totally flat.

There is also the question of atmosphere. Garden designers talk airily about *genius loci*, which signifies the spirit of the place. That dark holly tree that is a blot on the horizon may hold the key to your garden's character; without it, the job of making the plot interesting and beautiful might be that much harder.

The original proportions of old gardens are often better than later rearrangements. With some excavating, you may find useful earlier paths that have more logic than a myriad of new ones. Equipped with loppers and a chainsaw, untangle and liberate anything that you like the look of. Choose one good tree rather than three growing too close together in an island bed. Thin out that shrubbery, and grass over extra flower borders if they fill you with apprehension. Make the garden yours.

Above: A surfeit of yew trees, overgrown hedges, and avenues of roses made up this old formal garden at Glendon Hall. There was also some topiary of box, which well-meaning people suggested getting rid of, to reduce the workload for the new owner. She defended the plants, knowing that they carried a clue to the character of the place.

Below: An old yew was in the way here, offering shade where it was not wanted, and drying out the soil. On its grave is a circular bed planted with the more interesting-looking paper bark maple (*Acer griseum*), three tree peonies, planted alternately with three herbaceous peonies (the former being more structural and earlier in flower). Shade-tolerant *Veronicastrum* and *Dianthus* are planted in between with some height in the centre provided by annual sweet peas.

My garden is overlooked on several sides

In brief:
Think about how people shelter themselves from the sun and apply this to prying eyes

A garden in the city is a wonderful thing, if you don't mind being overlooked by scores of people. A light canopy of trees will filter views as well as light – a desirable situation in any garden. Japanese maple (*Acer palmatum*), saucer magnolia (*Magnolia × soulangeana*) and the more rare golden rain tree (*Koelreuteria paniculata*) provide dappled shade to eat under (or next to), without the bother of umbrellas. Some space is required for these, however. What if you have a small courtyard overlooked by hundreds of hotel windows (and I speak from experience)?

Roof-training is an ingenious way of providing overhead, horizontal shelter. Mulberry (*Morus alba* 'Fruitless'), with its generous, broad leaves, is shown here; lime could be substituted (*Tilia cordata* is a variety that is less prone to aphid attack, which makes the leaves sticky). In either case, a trained canopy like this is a design element that dictates the whole mood of the garden. Roof-training is a smarter descendent of the vine-covered pergola, not so much a romantic idea as an outdoor imperative in hot countries. With the help of a builder, a narrow garden could be turned into one big pergola. Wisteria would cover and hang, elegantly; the evergreen *Clematis armandii* has the advantage of good leaf shape and early white flowers. Both are scented.

Pleaching (often of lime or hornbeam trees) around the edges of a garden makes an effective hedge, with the appearance of being on stilts. However, it is costly and labour-intensive to establish, and leans heavily towards formality. For a systematic yet friendlier look, a line of country trees such as crab apple (choose just one variety) planted near a wall will soften the perimeter of a town garden. Be sure of their projected height, though: the canopy should float over the wall, not push against it.

See also page 52: *My garden is an awkward shape*

A sheltered London garden with roof-trained mulberries, designed by landscape design partners del Buono Gazerwitz. The variety is *Morus alba* 'Fruitless', which is just as decorative as white mulberry but without the notoriously messy fruit.

My garden is too small

In brief:
Think big; be ruthless

'The tiniest garden is often the loveliest,' wrote Vita Sackville-West from her writing tower at Sissinghurst Castle in Kent. 'How much I long sometimes for a courtyard, flagged with huge grey paving stones.' With her impassioned style, she claimed to dream of it day and night. This is encouraging: forget the castle and love your courtyard.

A courtyard garden means no lawn and many flowers. It must be permeable, with cracks for flowers to self-seed into, sending their roots under the cool shelter of the stones. There are plants that love to be walked on, such as creeping thyme, which also has the advantage of being aromatic. Away from foot traffic, there are leafy plants that hold dewdrops on their surfaces (*Alchemilla mollis* or succulents); there are spiky verticals and tallish flowers (*Sisyrinchium striatum*, or iris) that might seem counterintuitive but which remind you that this is in fact a garden, not just a yard.

For a small space that is not paved, the cottage garden is a good model. There is no room for design, just a need to cram in as much herbage as possible, on the ground and up the walls. Other small garden models to consider are the paradise garden, with its geometry and enclosure, and the Japanese garden, with just enough space for emptiness.

A small garden does require more focus. Choose only the best trees and shrubs, since they will provide much-scrutinized height and volume. Think about their silhouettes and leaf shapes. Simplify materials (paving, paths, seating areas), and make sure they relate to the house. Likewise, simplify colour, simplify pots, simplify garden furniture. Think of enclosure as an advantage, and add scented climbers by the back door and windows. Create a place where storage can be hidden, and use garden furniture that can be folded up and put away.

See also page 62: *Does a cottage garden require a cottage?*

A small garden needs an editor-in-chief to ensure that every element is worthy of inclusion. All decisions must adhere to the theme: making the most of a small space. A narrow choice of materials creates cohesion and emphasizes shapes and textures: the rounded, earthy pot next to the smooth horizontal of the steps. The brick used in the hard landscaping also complements the brick of the walls in this town garden designed by Nicola Lesbirel.

My garden is a car park

In brief:
It can be a garden as well

People don't tend to notice when their garden has become a car park, since it's so convenient to get the car off the street. This achievement blinds otherwise sensible people and it is left to garden designers to rationalize the space. James Alexander-Sinclair decided that in this garden too much car parking was really not a blessing. Plenty of cars come and go here, and the broad sweep in front of this family home with a pottery business attached is a tempting place to leave them.

James chose a group of four self-sufficient plants that are allowed to spread themselves about where they won't be trampled. Cars are directed to the side of the house; if they do stray into the view, there is plenty of vertical distraction, as well as wavy movement from the voluminous grasses. Diversion from cars could also be achieved with topiary or lowish evergreen hedging. In this garden, a line of pear trees is planted between the driveway and the road.

Gravel has its detractors, and, if you'd rather not use it, paving slabs set reasonably wide, the gaps filled with something well-draining, are worth investigating. It's a question of balance. How much parking space do you need? Older, more suburban houses were designed with a garage to one side, with a planted area near the path to the door. The front garden was a scene-changer between street and home, a mark of leafy civilization. Some people still want this and even go as far as to buy a resident's parking space for themselves, leaving the built-in car space for guests. The area by the front door can be as welcoming as this and, unlike a car, it has something interesting to say about the people living there.

See also page 68: *I don't have time to water regularly*

Gravel serves two purposes here. It provides a permeable surface that mitigates the problem of rainwater run-off posed by most off-street parking. It is also an ideal medium for undemanding self-seeders like these four: graceful yet wiry *Verbena bonariensis*, felty, towering *Verbascum bombyciferum* and the grasses *Stipa tenuissima* and *Panicum virgatum* 'Heavy Metal'. This planting does not need to be watered or looked after, apart from some gentle editing and thinning out.

I've spent all my money on the house

In brief:
You can make a garden cheaply if you don't rush

During building work, keep an eye on your skip and hold on to everything you can: old bricks, local stone, old doors. Look around at the local vernacular, since it's always a good idea in the garden to use materials that suit the house. Think about the garden all the time the builders are in, allowing it to percolate into your subconscious so that it will not be an afterthought when they finally go and the house is sparkling and fresh. Better still, take a good look at the garden before the builders arrive to destroy it.

While you are *slowly* considering your options, take stock of what is already in the garden. If it has not been completely destroyed by the builders, there may be plants that have value, given a bit of thought. The survivors may surprise you: bluebells, poppies, foxgloves, or columbines that have interbred and become a mucky pink. Dig out the best and move them around, remembering to water transplants in. Forget-me-nots (*Myosotis*) can be planted with alpine strawberries (*Fragaria vesca*) for blue-and-white prettiness in May and bijoux fruits all summer. Keep an eye on these easy plants, since their ambition will be to spread, though of course this is useful when you have no plants.

Plants are cheap if you sharpen your antennae. They may be sold by the box at school plant sales, or given away almost free at village fetes, having been lovingly nurtured in someone else's greenhouse. If you live in town, insist that friends in the country tell you about local fundraising events, and visit them from May onwards. Get in touch with other gardeners via the Royal Horticultural Society and local gardening clubs and plant societies (see page 139). All gardeners have too much seed, and they like to share.

One last point: a hedge can be grown from cuttings, once you know where you want to put one. Equally, its components can be bought in bulk as bare-root whips. They are cheaper and more easily established when bought small. Patience is required for this, however.

In both gardens, local materials have been used to edge the paths, with no investment in hard paving. Compacted soil can work as a path in dry places. Despite its English cottage-garden appearance, the garden above is in South Australia. The poppy border is in the walled garden at Wiveton Hall, in Norfolk, England.

17

Free food for plants

The only way to run a garden cheaply is to feed it cheaply. Keeping the soil in good heart is as important as filling it with plants and this needs to be considered at the beginning. The answer is composting: a convenient recycling system for garden waste and the best way to create 'black gold' for spreading around the garden.

1. A compost heap needs to be more than just grass clippings, with a good mix of green and brown.
2. Several bins are ideal, if possible. As one bin fills with new material, another is ready to go. This middle bin is kept well-watered and is a luxurious home for pumpkins.
3. Comfrey (*Symphytum* × *uplandicum* 'Bocking 14') is the variety to grow for making a high-phosphate 'tea' to feed flowers.

4. A quick alternative to the foul-smelling 'tea' is to cut comfrey (and nettles) down just before flowering and put the cuttings straight on to your compost heap as a nutrition boost.
5. *Trifolium incarnatum* (crimson clover) and (6.) *Phacelia tanacetifolia* make a bee-attracting ground cover where soil needs improving, before being dug into the ground and feeding it like regular manure.

4

5

6

My garden is a desert

In brief:
Beauty can thrive there

When emergency measures for water conservation are imposed every year for over a decade, gardeners take stock. Does the word 'drought' even apply, in a situation that could be permanent? The ravishing gardens at Lambley Nursery in eastern Australia are the result of comprehensive adaptation to long-term water scarcity, along with increasing heat (40°C in summer, occasionally reaching 47°C). In winter, there is frost. Although plantsman David Glenn grew up in England, the dream of a green croquet lawn couldn't be less relevant.

Not only are the gardens hot and dry, they are also exceptionally windy; the biggest wind farm in Victoria is a few miles away. Three sides of the property are banded by cypress trees (*Cupressa macrocarpa*); not a dense hedge but a sequence of exclamation points, 18 metres tall. Enclosing the area shown here, a wall of privet (*Ligustrum vulgare*) was planted from cuttings, taken from an old garden. No other hedging used locally has proved to be so long-lived. With this evergreen backdrop, the remarkable colours within the hedge boundary can really shimmer.

Plants have been gathered from around the world. Some of the most successfully tolerant plants have been varieties of *Zauschneria* from the west and southwest of America, where extreme drought is also entrenched. Bulbs have proved invaluable to David Glenn, as they have to plantswoman Beth Chatto, whose dry garden (see page 68) in eastern England is also home to lilies and a wide variety of alliums. Both experimentalists agree that soil preparation is key. This garden was dug deep in the 1980s, with a layer of at least 15 cm of new compost added. The plants were watered in very thoroughly, then watered again a few weeks later, then left to get on with it.

Euphorbia, lilies, a privet hedge: familiar as these plants might seem, nurseryman David Glenn only grows plants that perfectly suit the harsh conditions offered by his garden in Victoria, Australia. The unusually orange euphorbia is one of his own strains of *Euphorbia × martinii*, with seed heads becoming more colourful with age. Structural spikiness is provided by *Yucca rostrata*. The gardens are watered between two and four times a year, deeply, when the weather is cool.

My garden is a passageway

In brief:
Think of it as a stage set

A passageway potentially gives two vistas; neither one should be of a collection of plastic refuse bins. If bin storage is the main point of your outside space, construct a fence with a door to keep them behind, shortening the length of the passage. The quality of walls and paving is important. In the garden shown here, cleaned brick complements the painted pale grey walls at either end, which also close the space.

The grey wall shown here is covered in climbers. This kind of enclosure near a table and chairs is ideal for trapping scent. On the ground, French windows lead out on to paving slabs, but otherwise, it is a gravel garden. Gravel has the advantage of providing not only a welcome environment for self-seeding plants but also security for the homeowner, being a challenge to walk quietly on.

A narrow passageway is bound to have at least one window looking out on to it, so make sure the view is good. Here, across from the first window is a rustic bench. The second looks out on to shelves of plants arranged as a plant 'theatre'. These elements are framed with columns of hornbeam (*Carpinus*), which fares better on urban clay soil than beech. Like beech, hornbeam is good value in autumn, sporting leaves of yellow, brown, orange and green all at once, before it dries out in winter (new leaves in spring push the old ones off).

Lighting is important in a constricted space, whether as uplighting or placed very purposefully at intervals. Since everything is on display, choose high-quality lights. Twinkling water fountains and *trompe l'œil* effects are not necessary, just a sense of discipline and theatre.

See also page 12: *My garden is too small*

This northwest-facing sliver of garden is free of small pots that catch the wheels of plastic bins. It is free of clutter of any kind. Every element has been considered, with evergreen box balls to provide structure in winter and summer self-seeders in gravel, including white valerian (*Centranthus ruber* 'Albus'), lesser catmint (*Calamintha nepeta* 'Blue Cloud' and *Verbena bonariensis*).

I have room for one tree. What should it be?

In brief:
This is a chance for drama

Since it is difficult to imagine the eventual height and shape of a tree, a pencil and paper are useful when considering what to grow. Would tall and narrow (columnar) be more appealing than wide and spreading? If it will be growing among flowers, a tree with a light canopy is best: multi-stemmed *Amelanchier* and *Cercis canadensis*, both favourites with garden designers, have good autumn colour, and their airy silhouettes mingle with other plants. A tree that is more of a lollipop shape will stand out on its own, in the middle of a garden. Fruit trees have plenty of charm through the seasons: European or Siberian crab apple and cherry (*Prunus*) are hard to beat (though cherries can be very pink so do check first). Some of the most radiant orange leaves in autumn are found on cherries, while luminous fruit makes a crab apple great value from autumn into winter. *Sorbus,* or rowan, with its narrow leaves, carries exquisite baubles of yellow, orange, white or pink.

These are fairly safe choices. One spectacular tree can make a garden, giving it tons of atmosphere. A fluttering handkerchief tree (*Davidia involucrata*), for example; an Indian bean tree (*Catalpa bignonioides*), with its unfeasibly large leaves; or the wedding cake tree (*Cornus controversa* 'Variegata') shown here. These are medium-sized as opposed to small, but it does not follow that a small garden should have one small tree. Several small trees, yes: think of a birch grove or mini orchard.

Tree roots also need consideration. Willow will stop at nothing in its search for water; shallow rooters such as beech can disrupt lawns and undermine paths. Having investigated fully, plant the biggest tree you can afford. You will be providing a home for wildlife and shelter for yourself. You may soon tire of something mini in a pot.

See also page 94: *I want mature trees now*

A *Cornus controversa* 'Variegata' lights up a garden in May, even when the rest of it is also singing and dancing. Height is good, when the proportions are right.

My garden has no soil, just paving

In brief:
Pots give you the freedom to move your garden around

Whether or not you have access to soil in the garden itself, plants in pots add a different dimension. You can play around with height and scale; you can experiment with different textures; you can push all your pots into a solid block or spread them out at the edges. You can have small pots, of course, but make sure you have plenty of big pots as well, since moisture will evaporate from them less quickly and they will allow you to grow larger plants, including trees.

Some plants are better suited to pots than others. The elegant outline of hosta is enhanced when raised above ground level, and it is less likely to become ragged from the attention of slugs. It's easier to control the environment in a pot to keep it slug- and snail-free, whether with a sharp mulch, a copper band around the rim or the old-fashioned method of checking round the back. A pot of lilies (such as *Lilium regale*) by the door can be wheeled away when the flowers begin their long and lingering death.

Agapanthus will flower well only when the roots are crammed together. A fig tree (*Ficus carica*) will fruit better if hemmed in, and mint really ought to be, so that it will stay in one place. Frequently used herbs like mint and parsley deserve a really spacious container (for instance, a galvanized steel laundry tub with holes drilled in for drainage). A pot garden can support plant communities that wouldn't work in a flower bed; the plants themselves are the first consideration rather then the lie of the land. Blueberries, preferring acidic conditions, can stand next to varieties of *Campanula*, which naturally grow on chalky or alkaline soil. *Fuschia*, a familiar pot-dweller, can live near the prairie plant *Actaea*, as it does here, on either side of a paved area at Great Dixter. The freedom to move one plant around, from sun to shade and amid different shapes and textures, is an education in itself.

Displays at Great Dixter in East Sussex show that although some plants are particularly suited to pots, even giants such as *Gunnera* can be grown in this way. The shelter provided by their leaves creates ideal conditions for smaller plants that appreciate shade and moisture. Getting the watering right will come in time; just don't forget altogether.

My garden is too long and narrow

In brief:
Think of it as a vertical and divide it horizontally

Upstairs windows are an important part of the relationship between homeowners and their gardens, especially between November and March. They are perfect for planning purposes. It's useful to stand and think, looking at the effects of light and weather. This is what landscape designer Chris Moss did when he moved into the property shown here. He knew he wanted to create a curving path to make the garden seem wider, and that he also wanted one place to sit and another place to eat.

Chris already had a plan to grow vegetables, and they naturally went into the ground towards the back and in pots closer to the house. Light dictated that he grow food and most of the flowers on the sunnier side of the path, while curving, cloud-pruned box (*Buxus*) takes the place of a flower border on the shady side.

Dividing an imperfectly shaped garden is a way of obscuring its shortcomings while creating a workable space. You must be bold, though: a series of low box hedges will not dramatically transform your garden. An arc across a rectangle creates drama; a square within a rectangle creates a breathing space. From ground level, this garden appears to be a wonderful shape and size, its curving path leading away to who knows where. The texture of the sandy path (made of hoggin) is a good contrast with the smooth black concrete steps. In winter, evergreen bamboo combines with clipped box to ensure that this view is lively all year round.

See also page 136: *I'm not really a flower person*

A blank canvas can be bewildering, but Chris Moss has limited the options in his own garden to a handful of strong elements, including curved hedging, compartments and a restricted colour palette throughout.

I'd like water without a water 'feature'

In brief:
It could be just a large bowl
that is put out in summer

The first thing to do if you want to bring more wildlife into a garden is to introduce water. Just as worms miraculously appear in a new compost heap, the water diviners of the natural world will populate your pond.

Of course, they'd prefer a little pond weed for oxygen, water snails to keep the algae down and a few water lilies for underwater shade, but the concept can be as easy as this: one non-porous bowl and water. Dragonflies and water boatmen do not require a pump or a light switch that activates hopping purple balls at night. Water isn't boring: it's calming.

Visit a garden with a calm water system, such as a moat (or several, in the case of Helmingham Hall in Suffolk). You will be unusually aware of movement and sound, as insects and birds flit in and out of your peripheral vision, landing on flowers or flying up into the trees.

The anxiety deep water causes for those with young children should not preclude any pond life. A glazed bowl or sink that is teeming with fauna and one or two pond plants will have everybody gazing into it, in the same way as a good fire. There is a plant for every depth, for instance arum lily (*Zantedeschia aethiopica*) for a deep bowl of 15–30 cm, or Japanese iris (deep blue *Iris laevigata* for a medium bowl of 5–15 cm or *Iris ensata* for very shallow situations). Water lilies (*Nymphea*) need to be researched carefully, to match their vigour with the depth of water provided. For a small pond, stick to a small selection of plants and resist impulse-buying from a garden centre, while bearing in mind that pond plants can be notoriously invasive. For ponds in frost-hardy containers, a floating rubber ball in winter will help to prevent an overall freeze, ensuring that birds can still drink from them. Frogs will thank you, too.

Top up your pond with rainwater. Water from a tap will add nutrients to a pond, encouraging algae. Also, the chlorine in fresh tap water is unfriendly to wildlife and, at the very least, should be allowed to stand overnight so that it has a chance to evaporate. Follow the advice of Dan Pearson (whose bowl this is) and keep more than one watering can permanently filled. That way, water is the right temperature for both plants and ponds, and any chemicals will have had time to settle down.

We have nowhere to sit

In brief:
Convenience need not be the first consideration

The table by the back door is not the obvious place to spend time, unless it is gloriously sunny in the morning or catches the last rays in the evening. Urban gardens that begin by the basement often have a dark area surrounded by a high wall, with narrow steps leading up to the garden proper. It is probably the worst place to sit, convenient though it might be.

You may find yourself naturally gravitating towards the sun, especially at the end of the day, when the heat is less intense. A convivial group of chairs and a small table for drinks is all that's needed, though they may be in a surprising place. It's up to you to populate a garden; an expensive and heavy table will not be inviting to sit around unless it's perfectly placed. You might not need one at all, finding that something more portable will do, for moving around between lunch and dinner.

There are times when the spot by the kitchen door does work best, such as for breakfast when time is more pressing, or you are not ready to venture further. In the backdoor eating area shown here, the landscape designer Chris Moss has pushed the basement level further into the garden, creating more generous proportions for that area. The steps are wider, for perching on, and the garden boundary has been softened with wooden trellis as well as a low wall for oversized pots of evergreen box. Brick has been painted a calming black, the paving stones are random and large, the table seats six, and there is more seating on the next level. A bench is hidden against the wall towards the back, where people can sit, unseen, doing absolutely nothing.

See also page 28: *My garden is too long and narrow*

Find the bright spots in the garden, for sitting out in the morning or late afternoon. A place with a view is good for drinks, but if it's any distance from the house it will seem miles away when dinner is involved.

I have high walls and railings

In brief:
This could be your chance to plant a jungle

Given that rambling roses can pull down a tree after having attractively swamped it, a more suitable home for unruly climbers could be a townhouse. Rear town gardens can be as deep and narrow as New York City air shafts, or a section of jungle, with its deepening light levels and microclimate. A tall house front, such as the Georgian one pictured here, offers four storeys of climbing potential. Railings and tall dividing walls also provide an ideal framework for rambling things. Don't keep profusion hidden away at the back; let it spill out at the front.

Climbers that create visual problems in a well-behaved garden (jasmine too bushy, honeysuckle too untameable) are perfectly suited to railings and large expanses of wall. Lumps and bumps are to be encouraged, as one plant mingles with another. It is important, however, to temper this fuzzy greenery with something well-defined at ground level. The serrated, glaucous foliage of the *Melianthus major* seen here appreciates the protection that an enclosed garden gives (it is tender in colder areas), and the same can be said of the Chusan palm, *Trachycarpus fortunei*. How to mix a rose with a jungle? Keep to the profuse yet smaller-flowered types, such as *Rosa* 'Climbing Cécile Brünner' and *Rosa Banksiae* 'Lutea'.

Rambling roses don't need very precise pruning; they are better when left to ramble. If things get out of hand, prune them at the usual time of late winter or early spring. Take plenty of twine for tying them before venturing up the ladder. Vigorous climbing roses will also be at home here, running riot over the walls. This is not the time or place for keeping things perpendicular.

See also page 34: *My garden is overshadowed by trees*

The garden in front of this Georgian house is hidden, although it is on a main traffic artery through east London. Its co-owner, the landscaper Todd Longstaffe-Gowan, says: 'I love luxuriant tangles of foliage, and they've been very helpful in insulating our house from the din of the street.' Since classical antiquity is part of the atmosphere, a large fig grows against one wall, refusing to be flat and neat, while the evergreen foliage of *Clematis armandii*, with its jagged Grecian looks, fringes the railings.

I don't like gardening in the cold

In brief:
Prepare for spring in autumn, while it's still warm

Before gardening begins to lose its appeal in darkening early winter, there is often a long golden period: a summer bonus. This is the time to do the last tasks of the year before you go into hibernation. Plants prefer to be put into warm soil. Although they look miserable during the winter, the roots are busy and the whole plant will be at an advantage when the soil warms up again. Autumn sowings bring earlier flowering.

Biennials are another good way of getting early flowers, although by their very nature they take longer to incubate (they grow in the first year and flower in the second). Looking around in early spring, it's remarkable how advanced certain plants are: sweet William (*Dianthus barbatus*), honesty (*Lunaria annua*) and wallflowers (*Erysimum*) are all biennials. Self-seeders are also far ahead, having chosen their own time to germinate during the previous summer or autumn. These include columbine (*Aquilegia*) and honeywort (*Cerinthe major* 'Purpurascens'). They join flowers more commonly associated with spring, such as cowslips and primroses (*Primula veris* and *Primula vulgaris*, respectively).

Oriental poppies (*Papaver orientale*) are worth growing for their jagged foliage alone, though their flowers will stop you in your tracks in late spring. Reliably early and refreshingly bright are the varieties of euphorbia; their stature lifts the new season's garden off the ground. Bulbs planted in autumn will be popping up all over the place, some of them spreading if you choose those that 'naturalize' (such as crocuses, daffodils or species tulips). Newly unfurling ferns complement the energy of a whole range of ornamental onions, one of the most happily self-seeding being the *Allium hollandicum* 'Purple Sensation' shown here. Arrange spring before winter comes and it will take care of itself.

Shown here, *Allium hollandicum* 'Purple Sensation' seeds itself obligingly among *Euphorbia characias* subsp. *wulfenii* 'John Tomlinson' and emerging phlox (*Phlox paniculata*). The narrow leaves of a small *Elaeagnus* 'Quicksilver' provide a contrast to all the fresh green foliage, while a rogue scarlet poppy makes a welcome disturbance.

Large front gardens: what's the point?

In brief:
**Treat them as valuable space
for growing cut flowers or food**

It's amazing how rarely front gardens are put to good use.
Often they appear too large, with a long path leading to a
disproportionately small house. And if the back garden
is no more than a yard, as is often the case, that seems
doubly unlucky: plenty of room where it's least needed.
After all, who wants to relax in front of strangers or, worse,
the neighbours?

Hot weather drives people outdoors, particularly in the
evening, and it doesn't always matter whether this is to a
private haven or the street. Yet even social front gardens
look unresolved; they double up as surplus storage space
or luxury car parking.

The idea of 'curb appeal' has gained currency recently,
reminding us that first impressions count. It calls for
more careful consideration of the view from the street,
a tidying up, which is certainly a step in the right direction.
Real estate is almost always a part of this conversation,
however. It would be better to give appeal to your curb in
a more permanent way, with a good helping of love.

The past has some answers for this particular dilemma.
Decoration was never the purpose of cottage gardens: they
were intended for growing things. The sight of vegetables
in a front garden was not at all unusual. Before the 'Dig
for Victory' campaign in wartime Britain, cottagers were
already using every inch of available land.

These days, we are growing vegetables again and queuing
up for allotments (although the plots can be off-puttingly
large). The raised beds that cut across this front garden
share the utility of an allotment with the advantage of
looking smarter and being closer to home.

See also page 62: *Does a cottage garden require a cottage?*

A terrace built for railway workers in
London was extended by the addition
of this new house, constructed in the
same style. The garden is also brand
new. When the house was designed,
the owners asked the architect Sam
Tisdall for a vegetable area in front.
This was easily achieved with the help
of raised beds and gravel.

My garden is full of old rubbish

In brief:
While clearing it away, get acquainted with your soil

Your remodelled house, months in the planning and execution, is ready for its new garden. The builders have trashed the land around it, stripping the soil while bulldozing anything of value. Interesting but dangerous pieces of old metal and glass have been newly exposed in the process. The quick solution is to put down turf as fast as possible, to make the place look respectable. However, a lawn is alive, even when delivered in rolls, and anyone treating grass like a carpet is bound to be disappointed.

A more interesting choice would be to grow something that enjoys poor, starved soil. Obviously weeds, large and small, must be addressed first (see *I don't like weeding* on page 132) but there is no point in picking out every last piece of chamber-pot if you decide to have a Mediterranean garden. It will need good drainage (minor obstacles can actually help with this) and it will need sun. A wildflower meadow, the kind that can be grown from packets of seed, is also a good candidate for lean soil.

This is the time to take a closer look. Is the soil sandy, chalky or could it be used for making bricks? It might be more acid than alkaline, affecting your choice of plants. At any rate, after building work or long-term neglect, soil will be in bad shape and, for any kind of growing, it needs to be brought back to a level of good health. Building up soil with mulching material will create a new layer of topsoil, while encouraging worm activity.

Making your own compost is the way to start. Grow plants to feed the soil, such as comfrey (*Symphytum* × *uplandicum* 'Bocking 14') and nettles, which add potassium and nitrogen respectively; they can be cut down before seeding and added directly to a heap. For the easiest liquid plant feed, a wormery, topped up with kitchen scraps, provides instant 'juice'. Leave the tap at the bottom open, dripping into a watering can underneath.

Starved soil in full sun can be a gift, provided it has good drainage. It is more likely, however, to be compacted and will need to be opened up with compost, woodchip, leaf mould – anything to improve its structure. Use grit when adding new plants. Tired-looking soil, punctuated with rocks, is perfectly inviting to many plants. Fennel (*Foeniculum vulgare*), *Echinacea purpurea* and *Agastache* 'Blue Fortune' congregate in a garden designed by James Alexander-Sinclair, with *Salvia* 'Indigo Spires' going to seed in the background. They flower better in poor soil, whereas pampered soil would result in a rich profusion of green foliage and little colour.

Do painted walls cheer up a garden?

In brief:
Keep them strong and neutral, even when the house is a bright colour

A dirty old brick wall can take on a new identity after a powerful jet wash. If that is the case, leave it unpainted. If a bare wall is not beautiful, or is a mix of decorators' leftovers (including render), a solid tone can pull it together. If the wall is irredeemable, paint it before covering it with trellis, in the same hue. Unifying through colour is a good way to simplify a space, but be warned: a cheerful paint shade does not necessarily make a cheerful garden.

Colour depends on the quality of light. With solid blue skies, everything can be technicolour, in sun as well as in shade. In cloudier places, bright colours work when they are handled with panache, as in the wooden house shown here. It's a fine line: dark shades are more flattering to plants, whatever colour the house happens to be. Simplicity should be the most important consideration with hard landscaping, in paths and other structures as well as in walls.

It might feel counterintuitive to use a dark colour in an enclosed space. White is bright, but it drains the colour out of plants; black, on the other hand, enhances the structure of a plant, accentuating every leaf and tendril. Plants with good leaf-definition look wonderful against black: white or red grapevines, for instance, are fresh green in spring and fabulously showy in autumn. Try the dramatic, dinnerplate-leaved *Vitis coignetiae*, or the well-behaved alternative to jasmine, *Trachelospermum jasminoides*.

Black, or near-black, does need a lot of life next to it, however, and in a small town garden it can be too bleak. In the garden shown here, black is mixed with a little white to great effect, elevating a problem space while flattering the planting around and on it.

See also page 66: *Has decking been overdone?*

Above: In a lightly shaded town garden, dark grey suits the mood. It flatters all colours, including the predominant greens here, of the *Trachelospermum jasminoides* climbing over it and the balls of evergreen box in front.

Below: A magenta house in Portland, Oregon, provides a good foil to a green garden. Note that plants grow around it but not over it. Choosing plants that suit the conditions of a garden is sensible, while choosing plants on the basis that they don't clash with the walls is not.

My garden is an awkward shape

In brief:
Plant it as woodland

This garden is not only an awkward shape (roughly triangular), but also on a hill and loomed over by higher townhouses on the incline. In planting a grove of one type of tree, the designer Jinny Blom tackled several problems at once, including the need for screened car parking and sheltered areas for sitting. A community of silver or white birch, which leafs up early and holds on to its foliage until late in the year, filters light as well as views. The trees create a woodland effect without dense shade, working with the surrounding architecture rather than competing with it.

There are many myths about planting trees near a house, but the dangers are overplayed, according to the Royal Horticultural Society. The biggest threat is from a combination of drought, heavy clay soil (which shrinks) and old foundations. Since this garden was non-existent when Jinny found it, having been bulldozed by builders, the soil was addressed at the time of planting. Trees, in fact, bring benefits for houses, helping to both cool and insulate the rooms and reducing energy bills.

Birch is a good choice for multiple planting; here, it complements a strong planting scheme that includes repeats of tall, wavy perennials and voluminous grasses. The individual trees that make up a group like this are not as precious as one or two specimens. If one goes it is not a disaster, and they can have their canopies thinned all at once. This is an easygoing garden that can be left to its own devices, only needing a thorough going-over every few years.

See also page 10: *My garden is overlooked on several sides*

The smart design of this yard uses repeated verticals of white birch (*Betula pubescens*) and giant scabious (*Cephalaria gigantea*). Hanging over the wall, *Persicaria amplexicaulis* 'Taurus' (far left) and pheasant's tail grass (*Anemanthele lessoniana)* are joined by red clover. Around the edges, planted as a middle storey, *Buxus sempervirens* 'Bullata' is allowed to grow large and shaggy, a place for birds to nest. Three trees that were already on site were kept, because their diversity added value: native sycamore, hawthorn and robinia.

My garden is like a child's tea set

In brief:
**It will always have doll's-house
proportions unless you give it height**

A common error for people with small gardens is to fill
them with small plants. There is nothing wrong with
individual treasures in single pots: the perfect succulent,
or the antique colouring of a *Primula auricula* in spring.
Small pots can mingle with big pots in a garden of any size.

Go for some giants. No room for members of the artichoke
family? Make room, planning where to put the big things
first, anticipating the bulk (in width and height) that
they'll put on in one season. Tall, silvery cotton thistle
(*Onopordum acanthium*) is narrower but just as dramatic.
There are plenty of tall plants with a small footprint,
including *Thalictrum*, giant scabious (*Cephalaria
gigantea*) and plume poppy (*Macleaya microcarpa*) –
though they may all need to be kept in check to stop
them from popping up everywhere.

People talk about structure in a garden. Trees provide
this, as do evergreen shrubs, whether clipped or shaggy.
And, of course, an actual structure can give structure.
Given a light hand, a sturdy, good-looking pergola will not
look sorry in winter. Instead of the tangled bulk offered
by *Clematis montana*, choose something prunable like
late-flowering clematis, which will give you clean lines
during the dormant season. Annuals such as scented
sweet peas, tropical Spanish flag (*Ipomoea lobata*) and the
ravishing beauty known as cup-and-saucer vine (*Cobaea
scandens*) will give it a completely different character
during the growing season. We should be inspired by the
functionality of vine-covered structures in hot countries:
simple structure, simple plant.

For shade as well as definition, an avenue of small trees
works well. A genuinely large wigwam (not one bought
from a garden centre, because it will be too small)
supporting sweet peas or towering beans will raise the
garden from the level of the picnic blanket.

Above: Arches in the garden of
La Plume, in northern France, are
handsome enough when empty,
especially when complemented
by evergreen hedging.

Below: The pergola at Gravetye
Manor in Sussex was in the process
of being replanted when this picture
was taken. Traversing the path, its
bold framework draws the eye across,
making the view more interesting
rather than obscuring it. While the
planting in the beds prepares to
surge up and out, the empty pergola
promises another dimension.

I loathe orange

In brief:
Pre-conceived ideas can be counter-productive in gardening

When people claim to loathe orange (before adding red and yellow to the list), it's possible that a fear of bad taste is blinding them to the bigger picture. A denial of yellow is to dismiss cowslips and so many other spring flowers that sparkle in the early sunshine. The decadence of late summer would be sadly diminished without dahlias in every shade of red velvet. And orange itself does not have to be neon: pale orange, as seen on *Crocosmia* 'George Davison', is positively delicate, peering over a mass of strap-shaped leaves in fresh green.

All sunset colours go well with green. And foliage, according to some schools of thought, is even more important than flowers. The plantswoman Beth Chatto has been saying this for about 50 years, and her ideas, which sounded strange when new, have become widely accepted. With an emphasis on form, texture and movement through the garden, flowers take a decided second place, whatever colour they are.

Of course, not all leaves are green. Silver foliage is predominant in sun-loving plants (think of *Santolina*, with its yellow buttons, or giant, felty *Verbascum bombyciferum*). Some richly coloured dahlias, like the classic 'Bishop of Llandaff' and relations, are handsomely offset by their dark, almost black, leaves. Flower colour is just one consideration in a border like the one shown here. In a quest for simplification, it's worth noting that reds, yellows and oranges all go well together. There is harmony in a controlled palette. Add a strong contrast, like cobalt blue, and the sunny colours will begin to jar again. White can also be a troublemaker amid sunset colours.

See also page 64: *Is a white garden a cliché?*

The Cottage Garden at Sissinghurst Castle in Kent is also known as the 'sunset garden' and was designed for lingering in, at dusk. As the light fades, the bright colours glow. During the day the flowers are calmed with a generous amount of green foliage.

Are roses complicated?

In brief:
Simplify matters by sticking to shrub roses and climbers

Five of the roses in my garden are named after French *mesdames*, each with a distinct personality: there is a noisette, a damask, a sempervirens, an alba and a climbing hybrid tea. Put like this, they sound demanding, but since they are all climbers and shrubs, they really are not. Leave the ramblers, standard and bush roses until you are ready.

Although it is difficult to kill a rose through bad pruning, its blooming potential will be sacrificed. By narrowing down your choice of rose to two straightforward (and desirable) categories, you will quickly gain a degree of expertise, leading to better flowers. Soft twine, a pair of sharp secateurs and some loppers are all that is needed, besides committing to memory a few simple guidelines (see right). Having done this, pruning will become easier and you will stimulate growth, resulting in more flowers where you want them – which is probably not above the pergola, reaching for the sky.

A general, uncomplicated note on roses: it is most economical to order them in winter, as bare roots. Add some mycorrhizal fungi powder to your shopping basket; it aids root development and plant growth when sprinkled in at the time of planting, so that it makes direct contact with the roots.

Don't worry too much about black spot, but do remove affected leaves from the ground. Introduce ladybirds on to roses to keep aphids in check; if there are none handy, squash green- and blackfly between your fingers before they become an infestation. Feed roses after pruning them: well-rotted horse or cow manure placed on the soil around the stem (but not touching it) is traditional.

Climbers (above): Roses produce more buds when they grow laterally, trained on wires. They can be informally fanned against a wall, as seen here by the gates of Kelmarsh Hall in Northhamptonshire. They can also be trained in semicircles, with stems reaching up as well as down (see overleaf). On a pergola or tunnel, strong shoots can be bent sideways so that flowers can be enjoyed at eye and nose level. In autumn, whippy stems should be tied in to prevent wind damage, and side shoots cut back by one third. Keep the air circulating by tying roses in front of training wires rather than tucking them behind.

Shrub roses (below): Deadheading roses will encourage a second flush on those that bloom twice (this excludes many old-fashioned roses; do check the variety if this is important to you). It is also a way of keeping roses neat before the real prune in the dead of winter. Roses must be kept uncongested; dead, diseased or weak wood should go, as well as any crossing branches. A shrub rose like this *Rosa* 'Nestor' at David Austin Roses in Shropshire should generally be reduced by about a third every year. Then, every couple of years, select the hoariest, oldest stems and cut them out from the base. Do this properly, with sharpened loppers. New, strong shoots will be waiting in the wings.

Is a white garden a cliché?

In brief:
Make it personal, not an homage

Somehow, the White Garden famously created by Vita Sackville-West and Harold Nicolson at Sissinghurst in Kent in the 1950s has a stranglehold on the imagination. We can't get past it, even though other people do white gardens brilliantly in other ways, including the garden designer Tania Compton, whose garden is pictured here. Hers is actually a silver garden, but then, Sackville-West called her own a grey, green and white garden.

If we go back to the source (and there is no shortage of source material, since Sackville-West was gardening correspondent for *The Observer* newspaper), it is clear that the original impetus for the white garden at Sissinghurst was emotional and romantic. The glimmer of a white barn owl flying over the former rose garden was something she wanted to emulate in the planting: a glowing garden at dusk. A perfect spot to create a garden like this would be an enclosed space, by a building. This would have the advantage of trapping scent, making it the ideal place to repair to after a day's work.

Light from Tania's silver-leaved plants is reflected into the house from the north-facing courtyard. The white skeletal stems of *Rubus thibetanus* 'Silver Fern' have a lightening effect in the darkness of winter. In summer, the garden is allowed to ramble and range, and shaggy *Rosa* 'Wickwar' mingles with willow-leaved *Elaeagnus angustifolia*. On the ground, silvery aromatic plants *Helichrysum italicum* 'Korma', *Santolina pinnata* subsp. *neapolitana* 'Edward Bowles' and *Artemisia* 'Powis Castle' form yellow-flowered mounds in the gravel and between the paving stones.

As a standard, the White Garden at Sissinghurst has become a victim of its own success, copied around the world. For Vita it was an interesting experiment, worth trying, as she wrote with some acuity, 'provided one does not run the idea to death'.

The degree of white used in a white garden is entirely optional. In Tania Compton's 'silver' garden at Spilsbury Farm in Wiltshire, *Clematis montana* var. *grandiflora* grows around the door, and the rose is *Rosa* 'Wickwar'.

Has decking been overdone?

In brief:
As a style element, it needs to fit into the local vernacular

Decking is essentially nautical, like the smooth deck of a boat navigating choppy waters. As an elevation, it works brilliantly in the right setting: near water of any kind, in the woods, over sand dunes. That is why boardwalks look and feel so good; they are a lesson in utility, providing an efficient crossing over the untamed and unknowable. Where there is less real need, for instance in a back garden in Hackney, decking doesn't work so well.

As a hide-all or quick fix, decking is a little obvious. It is more effective when enhancing the scenery than when it covers something unfortunate. It is at home next to modern, wide buildings, the kind that look so perfect in the woods of America or Scandinavia. Contemporary houses made in clearings look strange without a 'deck', which functions not only as a big balcony but also as something more fundamental – a generous drawbridge that leads from home into the wilderness. Extended wooden planes, whether on stilts or at ground level, are an exuberant way of anchoring a house to its landscape.

Decking that is overshadowed by tall buildings in an urban environment will spend at least half the year breeding moss. However, it does come into its own on a roof, where the air flow is better. When smoothing over bumps and roofing felt in the open air, it is a smart option that has not been overdone.

See also page 100: *My garden is on a steep slope*

Above: The right deck for the right place: a house built among the redwood trees of northern California reaches out to them with its ample redwood decking. The view is grand; the deck is simple.

Below: In New England there is still a sense of wilderness, and of creating a human landscape within it. This strip of wooden decking in Rhode Island is a path but also a platform over the organized chaos of the garden. Jostling foliage is kept back, and a stone wall hints at increased order on the other side.

67

I don't have time to water regularly

In brief:

Treat 'em mean, but make sure that they are the type of plant that enjoys that sort of thing

The desire for a low-maintenance garden (and, let's face it, that's what most people want) requires a modified wish list. It's no good hankering after lupins and delphiniums if you don't intend to look after them, including going out at night with a torch to pick off slugs. There are many tough yet beautiful plants that put up with drought, flash storms, intense sun or dry shade. *Phlomis, Salvia, Bergenia, Eryngium gigantum, Gladiolus communis* subsp. *byzantinus*, euphorbia, grasses and Mediterranean herbs all feature again and again in the garden shown here. They are the kinds of plants that don't mind if you ignore them during the week or take a holiday.

The key is to prepare the ground as best you can. Beth Chatto's world-famous gravel garden in Essex was started as an experiment, on what had been a car park. After decompressing the soil with machinery and digging in compost to a traditional depth of two spits (two spade lengths), the plants were watered in for the first and last time. Chatto had to take extra care with her soil preparation because this part of eastern England is made up of sand and silt, with the kind of rainfall that gives it desert status. Yet the first word that comes to mind on examining her gravel garden is 'lush'.

Once shrubs and trees are established (this can take several seasons), they will not need to be watered much, if at all, because they will have sent their roots down to the water table. Self-seeded perennials and biennials choose their own spots by taking root themselves. Annuals that have been sown from seed will shrivel if they have been ignored, but once a colony of easygoing *Nigella* or *Bupleurum* has established itself, it will seed and re-seed forever. What *will* be required is thinning out, so that the roots don't compete with one another for moisture.

See also page 112: *My plants prefer to grow in the path*

Beth Chatto's gravel garden in Essex contains many silver-leaved plants, such as fluffy lamb's ears (*Stachys byzantina*), which are well adapted to heat and lack of water. Alliums are also high-performing drought survivors; the subtle colours of *Nectaroscordum siculum* join globes of purple and white around this garden. Thyme will form a flower-covered mat only with maximum sun and good drainage.

How do cutting gardens work?

In brief:
Along the same lines as a vegetable patch

While a herbaceous border can be a work of art, showing a grasp of the colour wheel at the very least, a cutting garden is the opposite. It is serviceable rather than spectacular, providing flowers to be taken indoors. Plants for indoor displays do not need to be grown specially, of course; good foliage can be found everywhere, in a garden or in neighbouring hedgerows (particularly irresistible when holly is in berry). A designated cutting patch, however, gives you control: you can grow what you like best, in any quantity, without worrying about upsetting the balance of the garden.

At a time when growing annuals was thought to be uncool, the British doctor-turned-flower arranger Sarah Raven began to persuade people of the potential of a cutting garden. It is now impossible to talk about cut flowers without mentioning her, since her persuasive way of mixing scientific thinking with an artistic eye has led to the idea that growing flowers to be harvested is a normal thing to do. This has gained momentum at the same time as a wider interest in growing vegetables, and the idea is similar: with productivity comes beauty. Divide flowers into families of the same colour; plant bulbs in trenches; don't be too tasteful; grow flowers to attract pollinators. Keep the balance in favour of high-yielding annuals, with just a few luxury shrubs such as herbaceous peony.

To an annual, which starts the season as a seed and ends it as a flower machine (the name of one, *Malope trifida* 'Vulcan', is a clue to its potential), sunshine is vitally important, feeding less so. The advantage of planning a cutting garden is that it can be laid out for maximum light, giving annuals enough strength to face the challenges of the growing season. Shading and crowding in a conventional flower bed puts them at an early disadvantage. In Raven's memorable analogy, planting annuals in this way is like asking someone to run a marathon on a water biscuit.

In the cutting garden at Petersham Nurseries near Richmond, southwest London, flowers are grown for events held on the premises. Late-season dahlias, chrysanthemums and *Veronicastrum* are grown in rows, with support from rusted-iron hoops, bent-over twigs and rustic poles.

I'd like a smart vegetable garden

In brief:
There is beauty in productivity

There are various terms used to describe a refined vegetable garden, each rejecting the humble ambitions of a simple 'veg patch'. The ornamental kitchen garden, laid out in a pattern and trimmed with box, couldn't be further away from the eccentric trappings of an allotment or community garden, with its own culture of repurposed plastic and CDs tied on string. While the idea of growing food ourselves is becoming more accepted, we still approach it with some apprehension. If only we'd listened to our grandparents. Where to begin?

Fortunately, the most utilitarian approach still reaps the most rewards. Growing fruit and vegetables in rows, whether in a raised bed framed with timber, or in rectangles cut out of the lawn, is practical and beautiful. Paths which are neat – and straight – provide all the design you need. Consider also the materials for supports, which can cost nothing while looking desirable (see right). Experiment with heritage vegetables and new hybrids, comparing flavour and productivity. Grow enough of what you like: bushels of peas, rather than a handful. Grow things that can't be bought, such as autumn raspberries, requiring no more attention than to be cut to the ground once a year.

Interspersing vegetables and fruit with herbs and flowers will improve the biodiversity of a garden, bringing in a wider variety of pollinating insects. Companion planting, a mainstay of the cottage garden, helps to keep a balance; strong scent (from mint, flowering alliums and members of the marigold family) confuses pests that might be zooming in on a monocultural row.

Keep certain things close at hand by the back door: cut-and-come-again salad leaves, mint, thyme, rosemary. Dividing and planting out supermarket parsley will keep you well supplied; leaving some to run to seed will keep the garden buzzing.

Above: At Monticello in Virginia, the scale is grand but the layout is straightforward, with row upon row of vegetables supported, when needed, on homemade structures. Shown here are climbing beans beginning their ascent (left) and salsify (right), which promises handsome flowers and covetable roots.

Below: The kitchen garden at Le Manoir aux Quat'Saisons in Oxfordshire is organized in a similar way, with produce grown for the hotel in straight lines. Everything here is edible, including the fabulously decorative love-lies-bleeding (*Amaranthus caudatus*), a source of high-protein grain.

I garden on rock

In brief:
Make this the theme of the whole garden

On rocky promontories above the Mediterranean, a surfeit of perfect lawns can be found smoothing out the hostile terrain. Far more congruous and self-sustaining are gardens that work with the topography, such as this one on the island of Menorca, Spain. Despite being remarkably bumpy, it has been made into a welcoming habitat for people, plants and creatures, simply by enhancing what was already there.

Cobbles were not designed for people in a hurry. During the time it takes to get from the street to the front door, this garden makes itself felt. Oversize rocks add drama, whether they are near the sea, on a moor or rising out of the grass in New York City's Central Park. They are untameable and should be regarded as immovable. There is life in rocks: a rock pool in this island garden is a local attraction for birds and tortoises as well as supporting the germinating seeds of loquat.

Since there is beauty in rock, flowers and intense horticulture can step back. Plants growing out of cracks have endurance, each one a paean to survival. These true rock plants are adapted to impoverished conditions: succulents survive on air and water, and figs, almond trees and oleanders dig deep with their roots. Sun is the other vital ingredient.

Where there is soil in rocky gardens, it can be rich in minerals. Take advantage of these rich pockets and use them for trees or prolifically-flowering blue *Plumbago auriculata*. Otherwise, an ideal soil mix can be added to raised beds, large containers and troughs with drainage holes. In a perfect rocky world, they will all be made from the same substance: rock.

See also page 44: *My garden is full of old rubbish*

Bare earth is punctuated with massive, immovable rock in this Mediterranean island garden, and cobbles, walls, containers, steps and seats are carved from the local stone. Texture and colour-wise, gravel should mix into this scene without introducing a jarring new element; this applies to all gardens, everywhere.

78

My garden is like a bog

In brief:
It's the perfect place for plants that must never dry out

While a dry garden can seem like an endurance test for plants, the opposite is true of a boggy garden. With moisture that is permanent and guaranteed, all manner of fascinating plants can be grown, whether giant, broad-leaved or psychedelic. This is not pond planting, but marginal or squelchy planting for specimens that would not work in a mixed border and are all the better for it.

Gunnera leaves the size of tents can mingle with the filigree verticals of royal fern (*Osmunda regalis*) and the bright yellow hoods of bog lily (*Calla palustris*). Flag iris (*Iris pseudacorus*) is just as handsome when it is not flowering, its sword-like leaves standing tall among the lower, broad-leaved *Rodgersia* and *Rheum palmatum*. *Ligularia*, its dark foliage highlighted by orange flowers, works only in this context: its broad leaves droop without reliable moisture.

Nutrients are in-built. (Heavy clay benefits from mulching but away from water's edge, since added nutrients will encourage algae.) Some of these damp-loving plants require shade; others do well in sunshine. Some don't mind, such as the candelabra primulas (*Primula bulleyana* and hybrids), in crimson, pale orange or golden *Primula prolifera*, aptly named 'Glory of the Bog'. The rarefied Himalayan blue poppy (*Meconopsis grandis*), notoriously difficult to grow elsewhere, loves a bog garden in dappled shade.

There is much to choose from. Foliage is bigger, sharper, rounder, providing ground cover as leaves unfurl. Stem colour is more of a feature, with bog-suitable shrubs and trees revealing a flush of scarlet (*Cornus alba*) or degrees of ochre (*Salix*, or willow) when coppiced or pollarded. Apple and pear trees thrive near streams and rivers that are liable to spill over. The delicate-looking bells of snake's head fritillary (*Fritillaria meleagris*), which can be difficult to establish en masse, love gathering on a flood plain.

Above: At Coton Manor in Northamptonshire, giant leaves of *Gunnera manicata* loom over a clump of *Persicaria bistorta* 'Superba' with *Alchemilla mollis*.

Below: *Iris sibirica* 'Ruffled Velvet', *Rodgersia aesculifolia* and fern *Matteuccia struthiopteris* growing at water's edge.

I want an English flower border

In brief:
Use three basic ingredients: roses, peonies and irises

The weather in the British Isles is more or less perfect for gardening: damp, not too cold, not too hot. Standards set over the last few centuries have made the English style a difficult act to follow, even in the British Isles themselves. While the dream of an unsustainably close-cut lawn lives on around the globe, it is the herbaceous border that really confounds imitators.

'Herbaceous' is a way of describing plants that are not woody: they generally leave nothing growing above ground during winter dormancy. A border that is interspersed with woody shrubs requires less staking and planning than one that is entirely herbaceous. One way of providing year-round structure is through evergreen topiary, stationed at intervals amid the perennials and annuals. In the border shown here, the woody punctuation comes from roses, which are grown as shrubs as well as climbers that cover the old brick walls. They are joined by irises and the occasional tree peony, which flower earlier than herbaceous peonies, followed by highly decorative seed heads.

In this narrow edit of plant types – rose, peony, iris – there is unlimited choice in actual varieties. With the repetition of shape and form, any kind of rose can rub along with any kind of peony. The choice is up to you. Iris can be pale, dark, bright or muted; it will never compete too much with the main idea. Iris provides an accent, as does the addition of a few perennials, self-seeding valerian (*Centranthus ruber*) and airy *Thalictrum*. They perform the important job of undermining the rules, further abetted by colonies of forget-me-not and love-in-a-mist.

The idea of colour in an English flower border has caused some anguish over the years. A classic Gertrude Jekyll-influenced plan would involve an uninterrupted sequence of colour from hot to cool, all flowering at once. A late spring and early summer border, like the one shown here, requires fewer choices.

The South Border at Helmingham Hall in Suffolk is fairly narrow, wedged between the kitchen-garden wall and a moat. It is a focal point in late spring and summer.

I'm frightened of wasps

In brief:
Don't let this stop you from growing fruit near the house

If you have an empty wall, facing in any direction, use it. A sunny or shady wall that is not beautiful can be disguised with climbers and vines but a lovely one is a gift for training fruit as espaliers. A wide or tall framework of blossom and fruit will enhance a wall without covering it over. Edging a ground-floor window and even decorating the upper storeys, it is hard to resist.

What about the accompanying wasps, though? They are attracted to all fruit trees at the end of summer, and it makes little difference whether you have an apple tree in a small garden or pears growing under the window (and pears do make very handsome espaliers). The same can be said about bees, which should be fine – unless you are allergic to stings.

Wasps and bees both react defensively to the alarm pheromones given off by agitated humans, so: don't panic! You are more likely to be stung if you do. The advantages of wasps are worth recounting, for those who class them in the useless category along with horseflies. Early in the season they are busy building nests and feeding their young on huge numbers of smaller pests, such as greenfly and caterpillars. They also feed on certain plants, pollinating them in the process. Only later do they buzz in our direction, looking for sugar as their nests break down. They prefer fruit that has gone soft, such as stone fruit or windfalls. They help with the annual decay, too: a wasp in a compost heap is no bad thing, although a very dry compost heap might be irresistible for nest-building.

This, then, could be the perfect combination: roses *and* pears round the door, with a plum tree nearby. There will be fewer greenflies on the roses and, later on, early-ripening plums will be distraction enough for the wasps.

Above: Pears such as 'Conference', are usually picked when rock hard and ripened indoors.

Below: Plums are far more attractive to wasps, being thin-skinned and juicier.

Are meadows difficult?

In brief:
Grow a meadow that suits the ground you already have

The idea of a meadow has a romance and a well-placed nostalgia: in the UK, for instance, 98 per cent of ancient meadowland has disappeared since World War II. As gardens are valued increasingly as ecologically vital pockets, more people are creating their own meadows, instead of hoping that the fondly remembered patch of rough grass, smothered in cowslips in spring, is still there. Some seed companies sell wildflower plugs, a simple though expensive way of supplementing a piece of burgeoning meadow in the garden, where a few species have already begun to thrive.

Adding plants to shaggy grass is the easiest kind of gardening. Plants that would need staking in a border grow 'hard' in these competitive situations; they are more wiry, less likely to flop. Weeds too, take on a different personality. A dandelion in rough grass is just another wildflower. Buttercups and daisies … don't these feature in the meadows of our dreams? Flowers can come and go against a foil of green grass – there are no gaps in the border here.

It's instructive (and fascinating) to take a closer look at plants that grow on roadside verges: they almost always have a smarter equivalent, bred for certain qualities such as enhanced colour and decreased vigour. So, you can have a low-key meadow by letting the grass grow longer and planting more wildflowers, or you can use garden plants in a wild way. The garden shown here is left unmown between New Year and September, after which it is mown several times, the clippings removed to prevent nutrition being absorbed into the soil. Grass is generally weakened by competition. To further reduce its vigour, sow the seeds of the attractive semi-parasite yellow rattle (*Rhinanthus minor*) straight into patches of bare earth after the first mowing.

Bronze-leaved peonies mix with hardy geraniums (*Geranium phaeum* and *Geranium pratense*), perennial cornflower (near-black *Centaurea* 'Jordy'), *Persicaria*, *Veronicastrum* and dark *Camassia quamash* at the edge of a 'wild garden' at Cottesbrooke Hall, Northamptonshire. This perennial meadow is mainly made up of leftovers from the formal garden.

How formal is too formal?

In brief:

**It's more interesting to use formal
elements in a relaxed way**

Too often, when people call the professionals in, the effect is of a tidying away, with an abundance of topiary and hard paving, leaving a horrible stiffness. Great gardens are never just 'neat'. They have soul, romance, a story. The Manor at Asthall, shown here, is nestled in the impossibly pretty Windrush Valley in the Cotswolds, between a stream and a churchyard. The house itself looks like a kind of fiction, and it is in a way, being the former home of the Mitford family and the setting for Nancy Mitford's much-loved mid-twentieth-century novels *The Pursuit of Love* and *Love in a Cold Climate*.

The spirit of the place was never in question, but the people behind this garden (with the guidance of design duo Julian and Isabel Bannerman) have heaped on more and yet more; a garden cannot be *too* atmospheric, when atmosphere is the main theme.

Relaxed formality relies on good foundations, like a sofa covered with old chintz. The style of the house is reinforced with ribbons of box, encircling it in neatly clipped swags. Against this framework roses run riot over the house, while spilling over boundary walls into the lane beyond. Lady's mantle (*Alchemilla mollis*), hardy geraniums and lavender are no strangers to the formal scene but instead of doing service as edging, they form clouds of acid yellow, magenta and purple in the gravel. Enormous yellow *Verbascum olympicum* pop up wherever they feel the urge. Self-seeders are at home here.

Unruly rosemary adds more wild energy to the aromatic profusion. This is a home that is not stately, though it could be. The architecture of the 400-year-old house has been enhanced with creativity. A formal garden can be a paradise; it just needs some attitude.

Above: At Asthall Manor in Oxfordshire, ribbons of box enhance the shape of the house, rather than pretending to be useful in holding back plants.

Below: Yellow candelabras of the self-seeding *Verbascum olympicum* surge up amid acid clouds of *Alchemilla mollis*. This is mixed with lavender, rosemary and hardy geraniums, none of them neat.

I want mature trees now

In brief:
Plant small trees, mixed with some large slow-growers

Planting trees is not a selfless act: a woodland garden needs less maintenance than a bowling-green lawn. A copse, spinney or grove provides plenty to look at, with no need for flowers (though a perfect place for spring bulbs). An orchard or mini-orchard gives a garden charm and character. To plant an enormous specimen takes guts, yet there is nothing like a large old tree to create a powerful sense of place. Trees that grow to a great size should be planted more often.

Although young trees are easier to establish, it is possible to fast-forward by buying something more mature. Craning in large trees is not unheard of – whole forests are sometimes planted in this way. (Note that larger trees require more care in establishing, including extended watering and feeding.) A quantity of trees, staked and fenced, is a lovely sight, with beauty in the intent (see *My garden is a field* on page 108). Young trees are best staked against nibbling predators. The whole of the garden shown here (facing, below) is surrounded by basic deer fencing, for the sake of the roses and vegetables as well as establishing trees.

Young apple trees can look unsatisfactory for a few years, producing three fruits from a twig in the ground. Trained against a wall or as low 'stepover' edging, they at least give the visual effect of going somewhere. They can be bought at two years old with training already begun, or as 'maidens' in which case the slightly nerve-wracking business of training is in your hands.

Enthusiastic gardeners plant trees because they love them at every stage. There is pleasure in slow gardening. The pragmatic and hopeful approach is to plant a mixture of large trees, which you won't see in their maturity, and smaller ones, which you might.

See also page 114: *I need a fast-growing hedge*

Above: A line of old lime trees that are nearing the end of their lifespan is interplanted with young specimens. To form a double row, oaks have been planted in front.

Below: The Siberian crab apple *Malus × robusta* is planted in a sloping garden with quince, plum, pear and mulberry.

My garden collapses after June

In brief:
Stake your plants early and enjoy them late

'Everything has lost that adolescent look, that look of astonishment at its own youth,' wrote Vita Sackville-West in a July gardening column for *The Observer* newspaper. 'The middle-age spread has begun.' A surprising number of people feel similarly deflated once June is over, as though the progression from midwinter to midsummer is the only one that matters.

It is true that things can become a little overblown by June. Wind, aided by trampling dogs and cats, flattens top-heavy plants. Staking after midsummer always looks like an afterthought; it's important instead to look ahead, much, much earlier. Use markers to keep track of where your herbaceous plants are before they die down in winter. When new shoots begin to appear in late winter and very early spring, build cages over them, of fresh, bendy twigs. These can be made of anything with malleability, from beech and birch to the more usual hazel and willow.

An alternative, or supplement, to staking is to coax your flowers into growing more sturdily. The Chelsea Chop, administered at the time of the Chelsea Flower Show near the end of May, involves cutting down summer flowers (by a third to a half), just as they are about to have their moment. This can be painful, so try chopping just some of them, giving late-flowering plants like phlox, aster and helenium a staggered flowering programme.

Dahlias, native to Mexico, are well worth the wait, with their delightful near neighbours *Cobaea scandens* (the cup-and-saucer vine). The decadent shapes of South American climbers *Ipomoea lobata* (Spanish flag) and nasturtium perfectly suit the torpor of August. Rich textures are joined by autumn colours as trees become interesting again; it's the best time of the year.

See also page 98: *There is nothing to look at in winter*

Above: End-of-summer gardens can be the best of all. At Glendon Hall, starbursts of *Dahlia* 'Honka Surprise' mix with pale 'Twyning's After Eight', sporting dark leaves.

Below: Lovely (and toxic) *Ricinus communis*, against a wave of *Stipa gigantea*, give the garden at Hemingford Manor in Cambridgeshire a more exotic allure.

97

There is nothing to look at in winter

In brief:
The garden will stand or fall on this view

Hardcore gardeners enjoy winter because they can step back from the day-to-day and do some planning. It's an opportunity to take stock, to look over notes and photos and think about the future. After autumn has packed its bags, horticulturalists seize the chance to plant trees, establish hedges and buy roses. Plants will need to be moved, and paths made. The structure of the garden will be scrutinized, as it is revealed for the first time in months.

This approach does not suit everyone, of course; many of us prefer to experience our winter garden from the other side of a window. For garden-gazers there are things to enjoy during this longest of seasons. Some plants look good all year round but take on an extra layer of beauty in winter, such as the grass *Calamagrostis × acutiflora* 'Karl Foerster' and thorny pyracantha. Other plants hang about all year, always the understudy, until their big moment: holly in its many forms; the black and red tracery of cotoneaster; witch hazel with its tiny orange wigs on bare branches; very fragrant winter honeysuckle; the rare and rewarding winter-flowering cherry.

A garden with good structure will not only be planned for summer but will also take into account the lighting effects of low sunshine and frost, later in the year. Grasses and desiccated seed heads are particularly good for this. Cut plants down as they really start to collapse, not while they are still looking interesting at the beginning of winter. Prepare for winter by mowing the lawn in readiness for spring bulbs, and mulching the flower beds and vegetable patch. Freshly turned compost is remarkably attractive. Then, when the first snowdrops appear, you will appreciate them as messengers of spring, instead of seeing them tangled up in the detritus of winter.

Above: There is a sense of activity in this kitchen garden, even in winter. Rhubarb is grown without light for a tender early crop, in terracotta forcers and under overturned pots. Different heights of clipped hedging, with domes of topiary leave a structure that is crucial; trees that are pruned will take on a more defined shape during these months. Winter vegetables include parsnips, purple-sprouting broccoli, spinach and some hardy lettuce.

Below: The red-orange stems of *Cornus sanguinea* 'Midwinter Fire' come into their own as the last yellow leaves drop off. Older wood can be seen to the right; it is pollarded for fresh growth, which glows in winter. In the background are the white branches of the ghost bramble, *Rubus thibetanus* 'Silver Fern'.

My garden is on a steep slope

In brief:
Avoid regular mowing and introduce some flat planes

If you've ever seen someone from the highways department cutting grass on a steep bank, you'll know that it's not to be tried at home. Grim determination carries them up and down an impossible incline, often backwards. It's all in a day's work. For unpaid garden owners, however, mowing encroaches on leisure time, and dangerous mowing will always be postponed. The result is a let-down, anyway: just green and more green.

It is more sensible to let the grass grow. How about introducing some horizontal levels on an incline, a form of cheap terracing? Creating more generous level changes can open up the possibilities of a garden. Any kind of leisure depends on a bit of flat space, so if you have none it might be time to get the diggers in. Broad steps, solid retaining walls, a flat area for games – all are worth considering.

When an old property in Lincolnshire (Easton Walled Gardens, shown here) was taken over by Ursula Cholmeley and family, the lawn descending from ruins to river was already terraced, having been mown for years into extraordinary neatness before being abandoned. The whole place was starved, with depleted soil, weed trees and an unimpressive population of fauna, mostly rabbits. Perfect for a wild-flower meadow. Plug plants as well as seeds and bulbs were introduced to compete with the grass. Now the Cholmeley slopes contain scabious (*Scabiosa*), knapweed (*Centaurea*), fox-and-cubs (*Pilosella aurantiaca*), lady's bedstraw (*Galium verum*), wild carrot (*Daucus carota*), wild marjoram (*Origanum vulgare*) and vetch (*Vicia*), all as interesting as their names and teeming with bees and butterflies in summer.

See also page 88: *Gallery of grass*

Flat walkways are mown, while the inclines are left untouched for texture and colour. Colonies of limestone flora thrive on the impoverished alkaline soil, supplemented by yellow rattle (*Rhinanthus minor*), which reduces the vigour of grass. The whole lot is scythed in July.

My garden is too big

In brief:
Find a theme and stick to it

It is difficult to define 'big', since for some people any garden is too big, with too many options and too many problems. Narrow your horizons, and think of a large garden in a similar way as a small one: it needs a tight edit and a big idea. This is a chance to develop atmosphere, whether linked to the house, to the area or to the stands of trees visible in neighbouring fields. The beauty of a large garden is that you'll be able to grow plants that come with the casual warning label, 'Eventual height: 15 metres.'

This is not an excuse for impulse-buying or trying a bit of everything. It is far better to repeat plants from the same group, boring as that might sound. It could mean lots of species roses – not boring in the least – or viburnums, which have plenty of variety among themselves: pompoms, red berries, good foliage, or crinolines of lateral branches covered with lace-cap flowers.

This is your chance to show plants at their best by choosing the most suitable sites available for what you want to grow. If you happen to have a couple of fields, as the English doyenne of gardening Beth Chatto found herself with in the 1960s, you can divide the garden up in a plant-centric way. Chatto's books *The Woodland Garden*, *The Water Garden* and *The Gravel Garden* are based on the variety of experiences in a single large garden in Essex.

Cover the ground with climbers that are also happy to spread horizontally, such as honeysuckle, clematis or rambling roses. Think of the future, and plant a cedar of Lebanon; bring in some peacocks if you have no neighbours. Also: get help. Whether it is your children's friends, an energetic au pair or a house guest who is getting in the way, make them feel useful and appreciated.

See also page 8: *I'm daunted by the garden I've inherited*

Above: Stag's horn sumac (*Rhus typhina*) is a tree that self-seeds freely at Glendon Hall in Northamptonshire. Edging a sumac plantation with box lends a sense of order.

Below: A large garden offers a good excuse to use big clumps of enormous plants, such as *Eupatorium maculatum*.

My garden is a field

In brief:
Loosely structure it with sheltering trees and shrubs

Which would you prefer, a garden that is full of things you don't want, or one that looks like a small bulldozed field? Or maybe your garden *is* a field, recently vacated by sheep. The latter is probably the more daunting situation: a wide nothingness.

Human instinct tends towards enclosure. A view is lovely, but nearer to the doorstep we need something on a more personal scale, to steady us as we look out at the wider world. This is not to say that we must box ourselves in, although a preference for yew walls was certainly shared by many garden-makers of the twentieth century. For practical reasons, shelter from the elements is necessary, and areas nearest to the house are the ones that will be lived in and used the most.

This kind of field–garden becomes looser as it stretches away from the house, with more closely maintained areas outside the windows giving way gradually to an ordered wilderness. With the removal of sheep and their search-and-destroy methods of eating, longer grass will allow naturally occuring wildflowers to grow, while attracting wildlife. Native plants compete with each other, creating their own checks and balances. Smarter plants can be dropped into the mix. The natural shape of trees and shrubs become even more beautiful when grown with clipped versions: box, yew, beech, hornbeam and holly lend themselves well to this approach. Earth could be shifted, using the surplus from a lake to create a viewing mound.

Within a loose framework, the field–garden will find its own pace. After the challenge of planning and large-scale planting, communities of large and culturally suitable plants will allow it to become a garden that is relaxed and relaxing.

Above: Not a simple solution but an interesting division of space, with mowed grass giving basic definition. Tania Compton has turned this field next to her farmhouse in Wiltshire into a fantastical garden to get lost in. Trees become patterns, clipped in different ways and set in circles or avenues. Clumps of euphorbia punctuate the grassy landscape with shots of acid yellow. Refined plants are dropped in among a mob of locals that love the conditions.

Below: A field in East Hampton, New York, designed by Reed Hilderbrand, stays close to its roots as former farmland with a modern building sitting in a modular layout. The scene is kept lively with long grass against short, the trees forming a partial screen. Minimal fencing cuts across the scene without interrupting it.

Can I grow food without digging?

In brief:
Digging is only one approach

Double-digging gardeners are a dying breed, annually turning the soil to two spade depths, with impressive neatness. Flowers are expected to behave, dahlias lashed to their poles with unflattering white string. There is a choice, though. In the 1930s, the Japanese visionary Masanobu Fukuoka came up with the concept of 'natural farming', which involved no digging at all. His ideas are still percolating into the mainstream.

No-dig gardening is part of a younger approach, although plenty of old hippies have practised it for years (see pages 138–9 for more information on permaculture and biodynamic gardening). The principles are so simple that it's easy to see why the old guard, armed to the teeth with insecticides, herbicides, artificial fertilizers and slug pellets, would hate it.

Instead of digging, throw a compost blanket on top. Soil structure is delicate and easily destroyed, and topsoil is where the nutrients and soil-improving invertebrates are found. Add to this layer, instead of breaking it up and introducing less useful soil from further down. The no-dig concept is only practical with a long-term supply of homemade compost; industrially prepared versions can be bought in bulk but will be ruinous, financially.

Think of mulching as a way of feeding and conditioning the soil. Weed seeds will struggle to germinate and those that do make it through the dark blanket are easily hoed off. Hoeing comes under a different category from digging, as does the use of a garden fork for loosening tired, dead-looking soil at the beginning of the process. This is when perennial weeds need to be tackled. A layer of mulch, then cardboard with compost on top, will begin the process of weakening even the most pernicious weeds such as ground elder, bindweed and couch grass, while providing an ideal environment for worms and invertebrates.

In the garden of the no-dig proponent Charles Dowding in Somerset, everything works together. A tall homemade wigwam supports beans over a bed of squash. The beans' roots feed nitrogen back into the soil, and the large leaves of the squash and other ground-crawlers, such as pumpkin and courgette, prevent the soil from drying out.

My plants prefer to grow in the path

In brief:
Perhaps they are trying to tell you something

It's tempting to ignore garden truisms when trying to forge one's own way. 'Right plant for the right place' sounds dull; it's more fun to do it your way and grow the wrong plant in the wrong place. After this fails you become better equipped in finding the perfect spot for the perfect plant. Is it native to the North American prairies? Does it grow luxuriantly around the Himalayas? You might think you have it all worked out, but then the plant doesn't cooperate. The woodland-loving foxglove seeds itself in a dry wall, or migrates to the hottest part of the garden. When vigilant gardeners move them somewhere sensible, they curl up and die. The fact is: plants grow where they want to.

Take note of where self-seeders spring up and keep an open mind. The quality of light, soil and moisture changes dramatically even between one side of a garden path and the other. If your paths are made of gravel, they are providing something very appealing: drainage and a layer of mulch. A pebbly blanket reduces evaporation and keeps roots cool. Seeds germinate beautifully in gravel, making a nonsense of carefully monitored, potting-shed propagation.

Is gravel the ideal growing medium? Perhaps, though light is really the most crucial element. Every plant needs the right amount during every season, not just during its flowering time. Moisture may be less important than airflow; received wisdom is definitely less relevant than finding out for yourself.

See also page 78: *I garden on rock*

Above: In this slightly shady area of the garden at Cottesbrooke Hall, formally clipped beech finds itself surrounded by pleasantly rowdy gravel-dwellers. *Sisyrinchium striatum* and chives dominate, while seed heads begin to replace the flowers of *Dianthus carthusianorum*.

Below: More spires shooting up from a gravelly bed, *Digitalis lutea*.

I need a fast-growing hedge

In brief:
Try to think about the long term

'There is nothing to be gained by planting fast-growing hedges,' wrote the legendary garden designer Russell Page in *The Education of a Gardener* (1962). I would concur, and add that the most famous fast-growing hedging material, leylandii (Leyland cypress), is not only difficult to control but also quite hideous to look at, feel and smell. Even after a trim, this lurid green conifer does not improve. At best it looks like imitation yew; why not go for the real thing?

If you agree that gardening is a process, with beauty at every stage, then a spindly two-year-old beech hedge striving to gain shoulder height will not concern you. For privacy, though, it may not be good enough, in which case a temporary fence could be put in place while the hedge fills out. A wattle fence is such a beautiful hand-woven boundary that you may be tempted to use it on its own, although it can be expensive.

A mixed hedge brings a country idea into a larger garden, although it is best used away from the house, being slightly unruly. Made up of plants that can grow into trees, set close together and adapted into hedging – holly, hawthorn and sloe – it makes a prickly, impenetrable barrier. The thorns, mixed with wild roses and viburnum (and with honeysuckle weaving through) are extravagantly frothy before midsummer. In autumn, the hedge becomes a patchwork of leaf colour and shape while bearing fruit.

A deciduous hedge is a more effective wind filter than solid evergreen, since it slows air currents down rather than forcing them to jump over and land in the garden. It supports more wildlife than a leylandii, too. For something more formal, traditional yew and box are still the best, as well as beech and hawthorn, which cling on to their brown leaves in winter, giving the effect of an evergreen without being green.

Above: Yew, a so-called slow-growing hedge, grows at a good pace, especially when fed and watered. Unlike leylandii, it will re-sprout after being cut back hard, and it is not susceptible to aphid attack, which can turn a cypress hedge brown on the outside while it dies in the middle.

Below: Young beech, shown here, could be planted in a mixed hedge, with whatever grows in local hedgerows.

I'd like an orchard without the glut

In brief:
There are many more benefits to an orchard than the fruit

An apple, pear or quince tree has so much character at every stage that it must be forgiven for providing a surfeit of fruit. Even in winter, a group of apple or pear trees pruned into goblets is a wonderful sight. Apple trees are a favourite host for mistletoe, and their branches are further adorned by lichen. Apples that are in no hurry to fall glow against black branches in the lengthening twilight.

Fruit trees give warmth to formality; even when planted in rows, they have a rustic romance. But then there is the guilt. Why aren't I baking enough pies? Who has time to prepare chutney? Enterprising farm shops sometimes get their juice presses out for one weekend a year, asking only that customers bring plenty of empty containers. Such collaboration is all too rare.

Crab apples pose less of a problem, being eaten by birds while still on their branches. This instant larder relies on no human intervention (although there is plenty to go around: crab apples make a beautiful, clear jelly). The fact is that some fallen fruit left where it falls also makes a good feeding ground and will not ruin the lawn. It soon goes, attracting slugs that are eaten by thrushes or chickens or, one hopes, hedgehogs. Blackbirds, being mainly ground feeders, gather under apple trees in winter, clearing up the ground. Apples that are kept in unheated storage can be sliced in two and thrown out to the birds when the ground is frozen. The empty shells of halved apples, their contents completely pecked out, will remind you that your thoughtfulness has been appreciated.

See also page 94: *I want mature trees now*

An old orchard in a private garden, where there is no chance that all the fruit will be used, even with the best intentions.

My garden competes with the view

In brief:
Think of it as a picture frame

In a garden with an amazing view, there is only one star: the view. Everything that is done there should be done with the view in mind. This is not a new idea. In eighteenth-century Britain, Lancelot 'Capability' Brown did a lot of clearing away of gardens while bringing the landscape (and its view) right up to the door.

It's important to have a frame, the intermediary between house and landscape. This can be achieved with trees and shrubs, while simple topiary shapes have a personalizing effect. Partially screening a hilltop view can enhance it; with everything laid before you, there is no mystery. A garden that goes around the corner, with a promise of something new to look at, is more intriguing. A panoramic garden is anchored better if it is planted along horizontal lines, with colour lower down from the house, and only hinted at from above.

There are other views beside the one from the house, including the one looking back. A house wall is the place for climbers, with flowers within sight of the windows instead of in the middle distance. Another view could be towards a structure, perhaps even a castle keep like this one in Cornwall. Giant spires of *Echium pininana* thrive here, creating a picture of further ruin.

A simpler setting, with a view over a field of sheep, for instance, calls for simple measures. The garden can easily borrow the landscape by reducing the visibility of barriers. A post-and-rail fence, kept free of planting, will be enough to distract from the farmer's barbed wire. Think about the purpose of a ha-ha, a deep, fortified ditch that enhances the idea of owning the view and a favourite technique of Capability Brown.

See also page 100: *My garden is on a steep slope*

While the purpose of Trematon Castle in Cornwall is no longer defensive (despite the cannons, which are carved from oak), the panoramic view cannot be ignored. With its ancient ruins, the garden has little sense of separation from the view; the opulence and profusion of plants in this corner of southwest England has been exaggerated by the designers Isabel and Julian Bannerman, who live here.

I am fed up with slugs

In brief:
Grow plants that slugs don't like, or make sure your ecosystem is in perfect working order

The choice of plants that are not attractive to slugs is fairly wide. A rule of thumb is to use those with shiny or hairy leaves (such as hellebore and *Alchemilla mollis*), those with self-protecting toxic sap (euphorbia) and anything with essential oils, such as lavender or pelargonium.

Timing is important with slugs and snails. Delay planting out seedlings until they are strong enough to grow up and away as soon as possible; soft young growth is particularly attractive. Vulnerable flower seedlings include zinnia, nicotiana, delphinium, marigolds (*Tagetes*) and lupin. In the kitchen garden, keep an eye on cabbage, beans and basil. Slugs will suffer the tough leaves of strawberries just to get at the fruit. Lift ripening berries on to a bed of straw to make it more difficult for the pests.

Simple, old-fashioned methods are still effective. Slugs and snails are easy to spot on a damp evening; they are also attracted to ramekins of beer, in which they drown. Surrounding juicy plants with a thick circle of something drying, such as crushed shells, grit or coffee grounds, can work. Though there is less evaporation at night, it's a good idea to water young slug-vulnerable plants in the morning.

Grown organically, healthy hostas are a great advertisement for a holistic approach to gardening. Slugs and snails are an important food source for birds, hedgehogs and toads; poison the molluscs and their predators will disappear too.

Some people swear by the expensive and imprecise science of nematodes, whereby slug parasites are released into the soil. Timing and weather must be perfect for the process to work. Finally, whatever you do, don't just throw slugs over the wall – they will climb back over.

See also page 76: *Will chickens destroy my garden?*

Hostas are notorious slug fodder, their bold outlines reduced to rags overnight. One or two signs of damage can be suffered when hostas (and other slug-attractive plants) are planted *en masse*, as in this Connecticut garden designed by Oehme van Sweden. The gardens at Highgrove in Gloucestershire, certified organic for over 30 years, are home to a National Collection of hostas (as well as to Prince Charles).

What can I plant instead of box?

In brief:

There are acceptable alternatives but decide whether low edging is really necessary

Box edging is synonymous with classic formality; even the Romans used it. Until recently, head gardeners turned to *Buxus sempervirens* as readily as a striped lawn. When box blight began to spread (through moisture-loving spores), from the end of the last century, many gardens that were structured around box were stripped of it. This has led to a looser style in situations where new thinking has replaced old habits.

Where a type of low edging forms part of a traditional design, it is possible to use alternatives with reasonable results. Sometimes a disaster can open new avenues of creativity. English lavender (*Lavandula angustifolia* 'Hidcote' with silver-grey leaves and deep purple flowers, or *Lavandula* 'Munstead' with greener leaves and paler flowers) is compatible with roses, its flowers giving it the edge over box. Tried-and-tested box alternatives include *Teucrium*, which has the vitality of box but is more sprawling. For those who prefer tight and upright, there is the shrubby honeysuckle, *Lonicera nitida* (or, as it is more evocatively known in America, woody box honeysuckle). It is an eager sprouter, even just after trimming, and it requires clipping up to four times a year. Some people swear by Japanese holly (*Ilex crenata*); others suggest euonymus. Rosemary makes an excellent aromatic hedge, from southern England to Morocco.

Yew is sometimes pressed into service as a low, box-like hedge, even though it naturally is a forest tree (as is box, in fact). If allowed to grow tall, both yew and box provide good, solid structure in the garden all year round, either clipped into straight lines or as bumpy shapes. This still works in a post-blight world, since it is dwarf box that is most susceptible to the disease. Cut leaves are vulnerable to spore attack and frequent clipping leads to denser growth, reducing air circulation.

Above: A low edging of lavender at Mottisfont Abbey in Hampshire perfectly complements a comprehensive collection of roses.

Below: *Lonicera nitida*, shown here in the Sunken Garden at Kelmarsh Hall, is a popular choice, with an appearance similar to box, particularly after clipping. Unfortunately, this needs to be done twice as often as with box.

I'd like a wild garden

In brief:
Aim for a slightly wild garden

An abandoned, secret garden is a heavenly idea, but when we do find one, the first thing we tend to do is tidy it up. In order to make sense of it, paths must be revealed and edges trimmed, since an unmanaged, completely wild garden is not a garden at all.

The idea of a wild garden was promoted by William Robinson about 150 years ago as a place where plants had some freedom, far from the labour-intensive and wasteful seasonal 'bedding' style so popular with Victorians (and still seen in all its glory outside Buckingham Palace). A wild garden was, and is, more 'natural'. Bulbs such as crocuses and daffodils get in the way in a flower bed, and look better thrown around in grass, planted where they land. Bluebells belong under trees, as do snowdrops. Plants that prefer space to roam unchecked, for instance honeysuckle, can find their way in a wild garden, interacting with other plants that have come in from the hedgerow.

It is possible to have structure in all this; in fact, it's essential. This kind of gardening has the potential to be a personal paradise, a reimagining of nature. A light hand is needed to create a dream of the semi-wild, rather than the nightmare feeling of being lost in the jungle. Loosely clipped topiary shows a human presence; paths mown through long grass make the picture look considered. Weeds are not prominent, although they are present.

No one is suggesting that all this comes right up to the back door. Gardens can become wilder as they progress away from the house. Out of view, a small amount of space could be left for nettles, which feed butterfly larvae, or log piles, which support a range of animal and insect life when not in constant use. In a more prominent place, bat houses and nesting boxes for birds are picturesque; bird feeders can be positively chic.

Above: Garden thinker William Robinson's 'wild garden' at his former home Gravetye Manor, in Sussex. His ideas about wild gardening, though not his exact planting plan, have been carried forward into this century.

Below: Bryan's Ground garden in Herefordshire. A mown path and loosely clipped topiary contrast with free-form trees and shrubs, and longer grass. It is an idealized wild garden.

Garden bestiary

Smaller creatures in the garden, such as insects, amphibians, birds and quadrupeds keep the cycle moving, by pollinating, eating and being eaten. Animal life in the garden is essential. Allow this to influence you when choosing plants and deciding how short to cut the grass.

1. Constructed houses for birds and bats should be hung out of direct sunlight. Something longer than grass underneath (such as the *Cirsium rivulare* shown here) will provide cover and a potential feeding ground.
2. A loosely structured log pile provides shelter for invertebrates but also snakes, toads and hedgehogs.
3. Ivy (*Hedera helix*) and grapevine (*Vitis*) frame a doorway loosely; ivy is important for bees, providing early nectar and a loose arrangement gives birds a potential nesting place.
4. Pincushion flowers (*Scabiosa*) are very attractive to bees and butterflies.
5. *Verbascum* is a tough plant and easy to grow. Allow one to be sacrificed to caterpillars (6.) so that the mullein moth can thrive. The plant shown here regenerated after a caterpillar attack.

I don't like weeding

In brief:
Change your position from defence to attack

A garden that is in good heart will not have a significant problem with weeds. There is nothing onerous about pulling out the odd interloper as you go about your business; a pair of stout gloves will do for a dock or nettle that has planted itself in well-conditioned soil. For weeds with really deep roots (such as dandelions), a sharp-pronged weed tool will make their excision a pleasure. Adding plenty of mulch to a border will create a thick layer that annual seedlings struggle to get through. Compost makes a moisture-retaining mulch; less nutritious alternatives can be effective as well.

Notorious weeds that thrive on neglected soil should be approached with a plan. Infested ground must be cleared of such things as ground elder, bindweed and couch grass so that the soil can be made 'clean'. A rotavator will only chop the roots into bits and cause a population explosion. If you are keen to avoid glyphosate (and it is no longer seen as the 'acceptable' herbicide), you will have to consider the long way round: carpet, plastic sheeting, anything that will keep light off the greenery, for a year at least. Even when the drastic treatment is over, it won't be really finished for a while.

At Gravetye Manor in East Sussex (facing, above), a weed problem had been allowed to develop over decades. Even now, having got on top of the situation, the head gardener prefers to grow annuals in places where new weed shoots might appear, so that the soil can be got at easily, and stray pieces of root can be taken out. The really noxious weeds are put on a heap that is burned, rather than on the compost heap. Finally, since weeding is good exercise and generally useful, it is an excellent excuse for work avoidance. In the words of Robert Louis Stevenson: 'Nothing is as interesting as weeding.'

See also page 134: *My garden is not relaxing*

Above: There is no room for unwanted plants at Gravetye Manor. Weed seeds will struggle to germinate when light is blocked out by more desirable plants.

Below: A dense layer of ground cover, such as the *Persicaria affinis* 'Superba' seen here, will act as a smothering carpet.

My garden is not relaxing

In brief:
Make a quiet area, preferably right in the middle

Some people relax by deadheading and weeding, taking stock of the garden with each snip or yank. For others, the garden is so alive with things that need doing that they are unable to settle down. If you fall into the latter category, share the garden and invite people round. Then you may be forced to sit and listen to compliments, accepting that the 'cup' of the garden is more full than empty.

A garden layout benefits from calm spaces. Take the one at Hidcote Manor in Gloucestershire, one of the most famous gardens in the world. It is divided into compartments, each with a unique and sophisticated character. Or Sissinghurst in Kent, which, like Hidcote, has gardens of a single colour. Focusing on texture and hue is one way of slowing things down. Both gardens also have this in common: open, empty space in the middle. No flowers, just turf and hedges. Grass and trees work just as well. A very quiet garden can be made of just these two living elements, but within a bigger, much busier plot, a central green chamber offers a place to breathe.

It takes guts to leave things out of a garden, especially if your wish list is ever-lengthening. A successful garden has more editing than a plant enthusiast feels naturally comfortable with. A croquet lawn, or another space for organized leisure, may be the only way to avoid filling the gaps. Otherwise, map out areas for different densities of plants, while standing firm in regard to the quiet place, which can be just as fundamental as terrain or shelter.

See also page 136: *I'm not really a flower person*

Above: A simple canopy in a meadow can be called a garden (and, indeed, this one belongs to landscaper Tom Stuart-Smith).

Below: At La Plume in northern France, a calm circle of yew in the centre of an intensely busy garden acts as a decompression chamber.

135

I'm not really a flower person

In brief:
Focus instead on garden structure, with flowers as a bonus

A garden doesn't need flowers if it has good bones. A grid of paths, trees and hedges can form a great garden, but each of these elements has to be wonderful. For hedges alone, this includes the clipping style and shape of each individual leaf. Without flowers to hide behind, every bit of texture will be more closely examined. The layout must be strong, too. Are you sure you don't want any flowers?

Planning a garden in monochrome is an exercise in discipline and it is a sound approach whether flowers are part of the scheme or not. Concentrate on lines and simple forms, from living things or from hard landscaping (paving, walls and structures). Then come the textural details, as well as 'garden hardware', for instance a water trough or oversized pots. Then, finally, colour.

With a green garden, colour can take a step back, although subtle blooms that hum with pollinators (for instance *Persicaria*) will increase biodiversity in a garden. On the whole, a green garden is a good excuse for exploring grasses and the movement they provide: gold tones of *Stipa gigantea* for oversized drama or the more compact and silvery *Miscanthus sinensis* 'Morning Light'. The angle of light is important so that grasses as well as ferns (like the *Dryopteris filix-mas* shown here) can be backlit by the sun. A middle storey of planting is provided by a small amount of *Aruncus aethusifolius* (goat's beard) with lime-green *Euphorbia palustris*. The alliums are *Christophii*. A useful and distinctively heart-shaped green groundcover would be *Asarum europaeum* (wild ginger).

Some people are so keen on structure that they don't like flowers to disturb the flow. Green flowering plants are useful in this case, for instance the acid green of euphorbias that herald spring, or the pale beauty of the stinking hellebore (*Helleborus foetidus*), minding its own business at the bottom of a hedge, flowering in a green way for months on end.

A garden in west London, designed by Chris Moss, is home to a good variety of textures both from hard materials and the planting. A tank made of zinc is surrounded by ferns, grasses and cloud-cut box, connecting hedge and wall. Green gardens need to have life and there are easy and elegant flowers that bloom in this small garden, worth considering even for the flower-averse. Globes of *Allium christophii* develop seedheads as they turn from purple through green to the colour of straw. The generous leaves of *Persicaria amplexicaulis* are embellished later with small bottlebrush flowers that are very attractive to hoverflies and other pollinators, while *Anemone × hybrida* 'Honorine Jobert' adds to the mix of leaf shapes, before its cool white flowers provide welcome relief at the end of summer.

Useful terms

Materials and techniques:

Annual plants grow from seed and complete their full life cycle within one year. If they successfully spread germinating seeds, their descendants will appear the following season. **Perennials** remain alive from year to year, flowering in the growing season before going dormant in winter. They can be evergreen or semi-evergreen, though most lose their leaves. **Biennials** are like annuals except that their life cycle is spread out over two years; the first year in growing, the second in flowering.

Bedding plants are frost-tender, grown under cover and planted out after risk of frost. Associated with riotous colour effects when displayed *en masse*, this style has fallen out of favour but the beauty and usefulness of more select tender and half-hardy plants should not be discounted.

Bulbs, **corms**, **tubers** and **rhizomes** are storage units for plants, helping them to survive frost and drought.

Biodynamic gardening is an holistic approach. By feeding soil, instead of always extracting from it, produce will have more vitality (arguably) without the need of artificial fertilizers. Healthy soil is less prone to disease. It does involve an awareness of and reaction to the rhythms of the earth: sowing seeds at particular cycles of the moon and burying preparations in winter. It does not have to be prescriptive, however; there is nothing wrong with being 'a bit biodynamic'.

Cloud-pruning is a way of cutting evergreens, following the natural forms of the plant. This leads to a clipped yet amorphous shape. Cloud-pruning is descended from Japanese principles; when *niwaki* is strictly applied the result is more theatrical and exaggerated.

Compost is a mixture of decayed plant material that can be made at home or bought in a sterilized form, with other ingredients such as sand and nutrients added. **Loam** is an ideal growing medium for many plants, with clay, sand and humus making up the main body of compost. A good loam retains moisture while allowing drainage, and contains a reserve of plant nutrients. **Leaf mould** is a natural soil conditioner and can easily be made by collecting leaves and allowing them to rot down in a dark, moist place (for instance a bin liner with pierced holes). **Peat** is an unsustainably sourced growing medium, with a stubbornly loyal following; **peat-free** compost is becoming more widely available. **Humus** is an important element of soil, containing nutrients for plants while retaining moisture. It is made up of decomposed plant and animal matter.

Coppicing is an ancient form of forest management in which trees are cut down to the base so that they will re-sprout as multi-stemmed smaller trees, useful as straight poles. A few hazels in the garden will provide a yearly supply of wigwams.

A **deciduous** tree or shrub loses its leaves in autumn, followed by a period of winter dormancy and a renewal of leaf growth in spring.

Espaliered fruit trees are trained against walls or wires, with branches spread out for maximum light and air. While saving space at ground level, this growing method is decorative as well as productive. Thorny plants with berries, such as non-edible pyracantha, can also be grown in this way to impressive effect.

The branches of **fastigiate** trees grow upwards, more or less parallel to the trunk. Cherries for instance can grow in this shape or as a lollipop so it's important to check the eventual shape of a tree. Contrasting fastigiate with clipped yew is a feature of formal gardens.

As an ideal, a **flowery mead** (also known as an enamelled lawn) was the medieval equivalent of our perfect sward: not green and weedless but studded over with countless flowers, as its other name, *millefleurs*, suggests.

Sowing **green manure seed** is a natural way of fertilizing, which has nothing to do with real manure. Having spent the season competing with weeds, when green manure plants mature they should be dug back into the soil to feed it (see *Free food for plants* on page 18).

A deep ditch reinforced with brick, a **ha-ha** creates a barrier against sheep and other livestock that is invisible from a distance. Popularized by Lancelot 'Capability' Brown during the eighteenth century a ha-ha running along a garden perimeter gives the impression of seamless landscape.

Hardy plants withstand the cold, though degrees of hardiness differ from region to region. **Half-hardy** plants (also called tender) need to be protected and should only be planted out after all risk of frost has passed.

An **herbaceous** plant (whether perennial, annual or biennial) has stems that do not become woody.

Hoggin is useful for footpaths, providing a permeable surface composed of gravel, sand and small clay particles. It is self-binding and less mobile than gravel.

A **hybrid** is bred to enhance particular qualities, for example aesthetics, whereas the wild (or **species**) plant on which it is based tends to be smaller, tougher and less showy. Species tulips are more reliably perennial, spreading themselves around and 'naturalizing'. Hybrid tulips generally weaken from year to year and need to be supplemented with new bulbs.

Spreading **mulch** on the ground is a way of covering it while providing protection from erosion and inhibiting weed growth by excluding light. It has degrees of nutritious value depending on its composition: homemade compost supplemented with manure or seaweed, for instance. Mulch is also used for its visual qualities: bark chips, gravel, shells. To be effective, mulch needs to be spread fairly thickly, so does not work well in an area where self-seeding plants are encouraged. A freshly applied layer in spring can revive a garden, covering the tired remains of an autumn mulch, which breaks down over winter and feeds the ground.

Mycorrhizal fungi are naturally occurring organisms in the soil which have a highly beneficial, symbiotic relationship with plants. By colonizing their roots and spreading out into an underground network they increase the effectiveness of the plant's root system in gathering nutrients and water. Manufactured fungal powder can be added to a planting hole. Disruption of the soil damages this network.

Permaculture is a way of working with nature in the act of growing something for yourself, by mimicking natural ecosystems. Forest gardening is a type of permaculture; instead of sun-loving annuals, perennials are favoured (this can apply to food production, choosing currants and nuts over tomatoes, for instance). Soil is kept moist with the help of leaf mould and worm activity.

Pollarding is a way of pruning to keep a tree or shrub a certain size; it is also useful for renovating outsize trees. It takes place in the dormant season and can look brutal for the first year. Shrubs and small trees, such as *Cornus* and willow, are pollarded for a flush of colourful, pliable growth that can be used for making barriers and garden structures (see *Ways with willow and other pliable things* on page 74).

A **shrub** is multi-stemmed and woody, usually smaller than a tree. Many shrubs, such as box, will become small multi-stemmed trees when left unclipped.

A **weed** is a plant that grows too freely where it is not wanted. Often, its rapid life cycle allows it to become quickly entrenched, upsetting the balance of other plants. These can also be filed under wildflowers, herbs and self-seeders, all of which can be desirable when controlled.

Resources

Useful organizations and websites:

The Garden Museum
gardenmuseum.org.uk
Though it is a museum, next to Lambeth Palace in London, it also comprises a national network of garden enthusiasts who organize visits to private gardens, with talks and tours by top practitioners.

Garden Organic
gardenorganic.org.uk
Charity for organic garden research, and home of the Heritage Seed Library. Organic ideas can be seen in action at their demonstration gardens, Ryton Organic Gardens, near Coventry.

Hardy Plant Society
hardy-plant.org.uk

National Gardens Scheme
ngs.org.uk
Its annual 'yellow book' is a treasured listing of gardens open for charity, usually for one day a year. Huge variety, from cottage to grand, but carefully monitored for horticultural standards.

Rare Plant Fairs
rareplantfair.co.uk

Royal Horticultural Society
rhs.org.uk
The main charitable body for gardeners, hosting the major flower shows (including Chelsea); funding research and education (including the college at Wisley and the Lindley Library); and widening its network of RHS and RHS partner gardens. The traditional horticultural shows at the Vincent Square headquarters are worth the price of membership alone.

WFGA
wfga.org.uk
A goldmine of information for the uninitiated yet curious, with work-study days run by head gardeners in private gardens as well as longer apprenticeships.

Wild about Gardens
wildaboutgardens.org.uk
An appealingly visual resource for encouraging biodiversity in the garden. A collaboration between the RHS and the UK's Wildlife Trusts: bookmark it.

And keep in mind your local gardening clubs: sales and meetings with guest speakers are good ways to track down unusual plants or well-grown, good-value plants, while learning about them from genuinely passionate growers.

Index

Voices

Gardening writers whose ideas and engaging communication style have influenced this book:

BETH CHATTO

Her gardens and plant nursery are testament to a firm philosophy, of using only 'the right plant for the right place'. This is not to do with aesthetics but with growing conditions, for instance only cultivating in shade plants that hail from a woodland habitat and are happy in a garden version of that. Beth Chatto acknowledges the importance of her late husband, the ecologist Andrew Chatto, in setting up the nursery. A passion for unusual plants defines the Chatto style, which appreciates their foliage as well as their outdoor movement. She is the high priestess of problem gardens, with a charming and unassuming writing style.

Books: *The Dry Garden* (1978), *The Damp Garden* (1982), *The Gravel Garden* (2000), *The Woodland Garden* (2002)

MARGERY FISH

Like most of the notable gardeners and designers in this list, Margery Fish had a facility for gardening memoir. Her transformation from amateur to expert is ongoing in her retelling of the triumphs and failures relating to the plants that she so lovingly nurtured. Her success later in life as an authority on cottage gardening is all the more remarkable because she was rather put-upon during her time with husband Walter, a retired editor of the *Daily Mail*. She was not a fan of the manicured lawn and neat edge, instead crowding her garden at East Lambrook in Somerset with a huge variety of plants which she nurtured into communities, within the setting of an informal garden.

Books: *We Made a Garden* (1956), *Carefree Gardening* (1966)

CHRISTOPHER LLOYD

A twentieth-century giant who casts a long shadow over garden creativity, Christopher Lloyd's lifelong work was based at Great Dixter in Sussex, where he was born. The gardens were designed by Lloyd's father with Edwin Lutyens, who adapted the medieval farmhouse into an intimate manor, with farm buildings, borders and orchards close at hand. Lloyd was not only a trained gardener, inspired in part by his mother's meadowy planting style, but a prolific writer of books and regular columns who loved to entertain and teach. Dixter remains a hub of innovation, under the guidance of Lloyd's head gardener and successor, Fergus Garrett.

Books: *The Well-tempered Garden* (1970), *The Adventurous Gardener* (1983), *Gardener Cook* (1997)

RUSSELL PAGE

His address book contained a comprehensive list of the smartest gardens around the world, to which he was summoned to consult on from his flat in Belgravia. Having trained in painting at the Slade School of Art in London, Russell Page added a painter's sensibility to an innate enthusiasm for horticulture and a detached judgement. His sole book is a complete education in landscaping, disguised as a memoir. Students will find themselves underlining almost every sentence and then, on re-reading, underlining the rest.

Book: *The Education of a Gardener* (1962)

ELEANOR PERÉNYI

A magazine editor and author (though this is her only garden book), Eleanor Perényi wrote the eminently readable *Green Thoughts* after exchanging the joys of Manhattan for full-time life on the Connecticut shore. Her gardening prime spanned the second half of the twentieth century, coinciding with America's love affair with chemicals, which was still going strong in 1980 when this compendium/memoir made its appearance. Perényi was an early convert to the organic cause and is never boring about it, even with the proviso: 'Readers who want to skip it are welcome.' A companionable writer with decades of practical experience in a traditionally laid out garden.

Book: *Green Thoughts: A Writer in the Garden* (1981)

WILLIAM ROBINSON

His reputation as the grandfather of naturalism is held high, by those who have heard of him. Through books and the magazines that he edited from the 1870s on, William Robinson suggested growing hardy plants in a way that suited them, while rejecting the high-Victorian convention for brightly coloured bedding. His ideas were appreciated at the time and now have more currency than ever. Despite this, his fame has long been eclipsed by that of Gertrude Jekyll, who wrote for his magazine. This might be down to writing style; she confides, while he rants. In the end, they liked the kinds of gardens that we like today. Robinson's own garden at Gravetye Manor in East Sussex has recently been restored to much acclaim.

Books: *The Wild Garden* (1870), *The English Flower Garden* (1883)